Memories of Great Budworth

A collection of memories of Great Budworth

by some long-standing residents.

Joint Editors
Alan Bailey and Sue Ritchie

Great Budworth Local History Group

Published by ~~ Nostalgic Books
Tel: 01606 - 891149 or 01606 - 891445
e-mail: books@nostalgic.co.uk

ISBN No: 0-9539143-0-5

Copyright © Great Budworth Local History Group

All rights reserved. No part of this publication may be reproduced, stored in a retrieval system or transmitted, in any form or by any other means, electronic, mechanical, photocopying, recorded or otherwise without the prior permission of the Great Budworth Local History Group and publishers in writing.

Front Cover: Church Street & High Street, Great Budworth
Back Cover: 1910 Ordnance Survey Map

Cover design and arrangement of photographs by
Tenth Planet, Whitley House Farm, Hall Lane,
Antrobus, Cheshire

Printing by
Alva Press Ltd, Ringway Trading Estate,
Shadowmoss Road, Manchester 22

September 2000

Memories of Great Budworth

This book was inspired by three former residents of Great Budworth who have since died. They wrote their memories of village life.

We felt that these accounts were so good that they deserved to be reprinted rather than only be available in rare separate copies. As far as possible we have asked their descendants for permission, and we hope that we have done their work justice. It is a tribute to their education at Budworth school that they were able to write such lucid and erudite recollections. None of the three were professional writers by occupation and all earned their livings by working with their hands rather than the pen.

Cecil Holden was born in 1896 and died in 1971 and wrote his account in 1961.

Alfred Worrall was born in 1904 and died in 1986 and wrote his account in 1984.

Harry Walton was born in 1903 and died in 1981 and wrote his account over several years, in the 1970's.

To complete the picture we have also included memories from seven people who were either born in the village or lived in Great Budworth for a long time.

The Editors would like to express their gratitude to all the people who have written memories and supplied information and photographs.

We believe that this set of memories provides a comprehensive record of Great Budworth and village life throughout the twentieth century.

The editing has been very limited and some of the memories are repeated by different contributors. Sometimes the stories are dated but we believe that this adds to the charm of the collection.

The memories have been compiled by the Great Budworth Local History Group and edited by Alan Bailey and Sue Ritchie.

Contents

		Page
1)	Cecil Holden	6
2)	Harry Walton	32
3)	Alfred Worrall	56
4)	Enid Kelly	94
5)	Roger Wilkinson	104
6)	Annie Littler	112
7)	Len Martin	116
8)	Mona Magnall	120
9)	Anne Scott	126
10)	Kathleen Harris	150

Cecil Holden

The first account was written by Cecil Holden in 1961. He called his account "OUR VILLAGE - GREAT BUDWORTH, CHESHIRE 1700 - 1961".

Cecil was born in Great Budworth in 1896 being the youngest of seven children to John and Mary Holden. In order of age the children were Harriett, Albert and Margaret who were all born in Wincham. Then came John, Sarah Anne, Arthur and Cecil who were born at 40 Church Street. About 1900 the family moved to 61 High Street. This was the family home for more than 40 years.

Cecil went to Great Budworth school and after distinguished service in the First World War became a joiner. He married Gwen in 1920 and they had 2 children. Cecil first lived in Comberbach, then Belmont Smithy, Warrington Road, then Hough Farm, Church Street and finally at Byre Cottage, Church Street. Cecil served on Great Budworth Parish Council for 18 years between 1949 and 1967 and served as Great Budworth's representative on Runcorn Rural Council. In 1962 he was chairman of Runcorn Rural Council. Cecil died in 1971.

The Editors

Cecil Holden as a young man

OUR VILLAGE - GREAT BUDWORTH, CHESHIRE 1700 – 1961

A Short History compiled by Cecil Holden, Church Street, Great Budworth, Cheshire

A fair amount has been written of the village of Great Budworth in the past and this lovely spot is widely known. It is a popular place for weekend visitors to the countryside. This writing has, however, been in the main concerned with the quaint houses, the Church and with far history. It has been borne upon me of late that there is a wealth of fun and information awaiting the chronicler about the people of the not so very distant past who lived in these houses.

'Every village has its characters', is a truism which, I fear, may not be true at all in the foreseeable future. Whether it is encroaching age or the stifling effect of commercial humour, I am not here going to debate, but it seems that the tales, anecdotes and bits of whimsy which I heard swapped and bantered about in my youth and of the happenings which I experienced myself seem to give another dimension to the characters of two generations of people who are even now still represented among us. It is, therefore, with a desire to leave some measure of this dimension, which is so hard to evoke purely by imagination, that I set pen to paper.

What I write will sometimes be apocryphal but more often factual, my method is simply this, to show the reader around the district and as we look at our familiar houses recall here and there a disreputable, or otherwise noteworthy, former tenant.

Absit Invidia.

Let us begin by approaching the village along the main Warrington - Northwich road. We shall pass on the left Belmont Hall, now a school, on the right Brownslow Farm and a few yards brings us to Fairfield Cottage - a lovely old stone-based and half-timbered house, which probably got its name because the cattle fairs were held in a nearby field. These took place on the 13th February, 5th April and 2nd October each year. Opposite is the Old Belmont Smithy, the workshop, now silent, still remains fronting the road. Next is the Cock Inn, a large and fine old pub, the poet and wanderer Drunken Barnaby stayed here awhile and wrote some verse. There was a painting of him, dead drunk, being assisted to his couch and on this picture was some of his verse regarding the potency of the brew.

Continue straight on, you will pass a trim house on the left called 'Little Dene', on an old map in my possession it is called Pinfold Cottage. Opposite lives 'Four Gill Thompson', a bricklayer on the Belmont estate, who was told at school that there were those many to the pint, he tried his best to get this measure accepted in the Cock but without any luck. However, apart from having such a distinctive nickname, Mr. Thompson was widely renowned as a marvellous skater. In the days when frost was frost and the Mere froze over, he delighted everyone by his grace, usually skating with his hands in his pockets.

A few yards on and we come to Cock Lane Farm, here many years ago, Alice Anne was housekeeper and young Joe Scott at the same time did errands. One of Joe's favourite pastimes was pulling Alice Anne's leg. Once, coming back from an errand, he reported, *"Mrs. Ussher"*, of Dene House, opposite, *"has been foully murdered."*
"Good God, what a crime and who's the guilty culprit?"
"I don't know, they got in through a window, broken on both sides, they got a brick for evidence."

Dene House is a fine building with lovely gardens. I remember a certain carol singing expedition, we had done our utmost for Mr. and Mrs. Ussher, rung the bell and waited, the door was eventually opened by a footman who rewarded us with, *"My people have gone to Egypt"*.

Down the hill, Cock Lane, until you come to Dene Cottages, stay a moment, on the front is some verse by the Cheshire poet, R E Warburton, as follows:

> Take thy calling thankfullie,
> Love thy neighbour, neighbourlie
> Shun the road to beggarie.

A few yards on, at the foot of the hill and we are at th' bottom 'uth' Dene. The hill leading to the village you see, is called Dene Hill; the one opposite is 'Goody's Brew', probably originally Goodier's Brow. Inside the fine old pump house runs a never-ending stream of water, icy cold always, even on the hottest summer day. Over the water pipe is a pleasant verse, again by R E Warburton. A card of a photograph of the verse is obtainable at the Post Office.

The road down towards Northwich is called the Wash because it was once flooded.

Before ascending the hill to the village I will write a little of its past. The village of Great Budworth takes its name from the old Saxon words Bode, which signifies a dwelling, and Worth, a place by the water, and so is the village, situated on a hill near two large meres, Budworth Mere and Pickmere. Great Budworth is one of the most extensive parishes in the county, extending into the three Hundreds of Bucklow, Eddisbury and Northwich. In 1851 the entire parish contained 3739 houses and 17990 inhabitants, of whom 9103 were males and 8889 females.

Of earlier times the historian, Leycester, writes, 'In the reign of William the Conqueror, William Fitz Nigel, Baron of Halton, held the village for Hugh, Earl of Chester'. In the beginning of Henry III's reign, 'Geoffrey, son of Adam de Dutton was possessed of this town'.

The village is one of the finest examples of a mediaeval village in the country, the fine old Church, from its elevated position, is a conspicuous object for many miles; but more of the Church later.

Now, we will ascend the hill but, before continuing up the main High Street, turn right up what is known as 'The Mount'. Down here when bikes were new and bore no brakes, tore a young man, I think of the family of Curbishley, full tilt at the bottom into the lady of the Manor; from Arley to greet the dames. A fine to-do.

Ted Vennables lived up here; known as 'Belly Likely', a remark that was his constant companion. At one time he had trouble with his sister, who housekept, on account of his returning late for dinner fairly regularly. She refused to cook any more dinners. Ted, a bricklayer, nailed up the lavatory door, saying,

"No dinner, no need for the lavatory".

His sister retaliated by locking him out of the house, Ted fumed and raged and yelled,

"Where's my b...y brit 'ammer, I'll knock the b...y hout down, and dress the brit".

One 'Barber' of The Mount, a farm worker, in reply to his boss's remark on the fine weather, said,

"Very good, few days of this in a week, ' be better than a fortnight 'ud do in a month".

The Mount is a pleasant place of old world cottages and at the end is a view of the vale between the village and Northwich.

Retrace our steps and we start on the village proper. Opposite the entrance to the Mount stands a nice old cottage but I should mention that formerly, before this, at the top of the hill and set in what is now the sandstone wall, stood the house of correction. Bad lads and anyone guilty of improper behaviour was kept there. At that time there was

Albert and Cecil Holden outside 61 High Street, circa 1910

no local police force as we know it today.

Next to the cottage stands a large house in which the writer was reared, a field behind was used for the village football. The visiting teams used to strip in our wash-house. I remember when Barnton Church lads were playing us, not long after the game had started, one of the Barnton lads returned with his shin very bloody indeed. My mother was very sympathetic and sentenced the culprit to suspension, castigation, etc. At half-time the players returned and the wounded footballer pointed out the offender – it was my brother Albert.

A few yards further on, still on the left, is a stone-based half-timbered cottage, it bears the date 1716 AD, carved over the door. It was originally a small farm and the farm buildings still remain at the rear.

Opposite is a red brick house, typical of Arley estate architecture, the home of our oldest resident and a descendant of a very old Budworth family, Mr Sam Worrall. Over 80 years of age, Sam is very active – I remember his father, bearded and very drole.

Next to this is a nice half-timbered house. Years ago it was a grocer's shop with large bake ovens at the rear. This was the first of the four shops in the village at the time. It was kept by the Adair family who still live in the house. It was the job of the young Adairs to deliver the bread. One day Mrs Adair received a complaint about a loaf being dirty. Enquiring of her son how this circumstance could have come about, the lad explained that he had met 'Mr George' (George Warburton of Sandicroft) and had to put the bread down on the ground so that he could raise his hat.

A little further on, on the right, is the Post Office and the general stores kept by Mr and Mrs L and D Burrell. The writer remembers years ago the shop being kept by Mr George Percival, and the saying was that George would cut a toffee in half if the scales went down too quickly.

Next door, hidden in the corner, is the house in which lives 'Matty' Moores, a great character as he grows older. I like the story about Matty arriving at the George and Dragon from Comberbach to find it lit up with candles, *"What's the trouble?"*, asked Matt. *"Electric's gone off"*, said Cedric Manley. *"That's funny"*, Matt said, *"the lights were on on the bus I came down on."*

A little further on, on the right, is the Old Saracen's Head, a fine old half-timbered house, at one time years ago, a public house. Until a short time ago it was a farm house – Mr F Renshaw, who died here a short time ago, was the last farmer in the district to use heavy horses on the land. He was one of the old village types, none, I fear, to take their place.

The yard to the rear of Saracen's Head Farm was called, in my youth, Porter's Yard, after the tenant of the farm, 'Boss Porter'.

The house at the bottom of the yard was at the same time occupied by a Mr James Hughes. He was very clever with the training of dogs, and would take a farmer's dog or any other dog and train it to do amazing things. I remember one Saturday night, one or two of us called at the 'Witch and Devil' (proper name 'Townsend Arms'), the pub stood near the junction of Marbury Lane and the Marston-Northwich road. This was the last chance, after leaving town, for fortifying oneself for the walk across Farish's fields to Budworth. Now Jim happened to be there with a dog he was training and an argument started about the dog's abilities. Jim said,

"All right, I'll leave my parcel on this seat and just before I reach Great Budworth I'll send the dog back for it" and that's how it was – the dog returned and collected the parcel.

Now I remember, either George or Fred Astles, our neighbour's lads, were given what was in life a very savage black Retriever. It was, of course, dead and stuffed by the time they got it – a lovely job, on its stomach with paws crossed in front. The Astles boy put it in a kennel in the yard. If it had been alive salesmen and rag and bone merchants could not have been more on the alert. Anyway, he asked Jim Hughes if he thought he could train it for him. Jim studied it for a while, speaking to it and the usual procedure and, after a while, said,

"I'm not at all sure that the b...s blinked yet" and, of course, that was it.

One of Mr Hughes's daughters still lives in the same cottage down what is now known to younger people as Renshaw's yard.

Next, on the same side is Noah's Ark, fronted by lime trees and next to this a pair of semi-detached cottages, the second of which – the one further from Noah's Ark – was the old police house. Dividing the two cottages now is the old retention cell, usually the offender was kept in the cell for one night only and taken to Northwich the next day.

We come now to what was another of the old pubs, the White Hart. It is now a farm and next on the same side we have the Vicarage, a large but neat stone-fronted house. The Rev E H Carew is the vicar. Since starting to write this book I have been informed that our vicar is leaving. Well, I have served under five already and not until they are dead or leave the parish do they have any good points, so the present vicar, whoever he may be, is always much worse than the last. In one parish I know, the old man asked that he might be buried under the mat just inside the church door so that everyone could wipe their feet on him. They had, he thought, tried to do just that all the years he had been their vicar. I must add that during the present vicar's eight years with us the services have been taken as I think they should be taken in the Church of England.

On the left side of the street now, from the Old Hall, the houses look much more trim. They were, I am told, re-fronted in the 1800s. I personally have carried out repair work and alterations at different times and I should say they are much older than they look. In the last of the four as you proceed up the street, lived many years ago, the widow Bebbington and, if we boys had nothing much to do, we would go soul caking to Mrs Bebbington. I well remember the procedure. We would sing and Mrs Bebbington would come to the door carrying a lantern - the passage was rather dark as there was no electricity in those days. She would say it was not All Souls' Eve and, as we stood our ground, she would return to the back living room and return again with an Almanac and point out the date to us. Then she would go back down the passage again to reappear with some apples – a lovely and kind old lady.

Standing by itself a few yards on is the Poplars, the home of Mr H Walton, a well-known person indeed. Next is the Manor House and surgery, at one time residence of the doctor and next to this is the George and Dragon, a fine country pub. Kept by Mr Cedric Manley, over the entrance door in the porch is inscribed

'As Saint George in armed array,
Doth the fiery dragon slay,
so mayest thou with might no less,
slay that dragon drunkenness'.

Also worthy of note is the fine wrought iron sign with Saint George in combat with the dragon. It was made at Arley Smithy by a local man.

The George & Dragon sign

I should, I think, mention some of the fun that used to follow a few drinks at the George and Dragon. Apart from special occasions, we could count on a scrap after turning out time on most Sunday afternoons. More often than not it was the same Irish labourers from outlying farms. I remember a few – Black Mick, a big, strong, dark-haired chap, Wiggy Kelly who wore a wig and after the scrap it was usually off. His head was like a billiard ball. Also, Walter Kelly, Old Fowler and the visitors from Northwich, Larry Tracey and Martin Dwyer, to mention only a few. Now I often wonder, was the beer very strong in those days? One never sees, or very rarely sees, any trouble after the sessions nowadays. Everyone seems capable of good conduct. Anyway, we don't get so many Irish labourers coming now during the early potato season – then most of the early spuds were lifted by these men with a fork.

Now, a special occasion I remember – I was only a boy at the time and took no part. The organiser was our next door neighbour at the time, Mr Jones. There had been a little spate of dust-ups between the Budworth and Irish men. Now Mr Jones arranged that the first night there was a reasonable number of Irish chaps in the George, some of the locals would leave the pub early and with suitable weapons take up positions in various doorways - the entry by the Hearst House, the School gateway, etc, - and when the visitors were on their way down School Lane they were to be attacked from the rear by the locals left in the pub. Then, to complete the Budworth edition of the Glencoe Massacre, the savage beserkers were to jump out with a surprise attack and victory would be complete.

As I said, I took no part in the affair, which I understand went off according to plan, with one exception. The locals re-assembled to call the roll outside the pub and to laugh over the punishment handed out. I think it was Mr Jones who said,

"I didn't half wallop one poor devil in Martha Scott's doorway".
A voice replied, *"It was me you damn fool, I hadn't time to get ready".*

All this may seem rather tough on the visitors but I think the present set-up with razor blades, etc is far worse.

How gradually and easily names of places change. For instance, what is now the George and Dragon car park was years ago called Wright's sands. Well, I can understand Wright's – W Wright kept the George and Dragon, but sands beats me – probably the patch was surfaced by small bricks with a topping of sand. However, it was here I remember the local members of the Cheshire Yeomanry met occasionally and were put through their paces by Sergeant Cox. They looked very smart. It was the custom of the large tenant farmers to supply both a man and a horse, the small farmer, either a man or a horse. I remember my father telling me once of the time when Sergeant Cox ordered, *"Draw swords".*

"What, now sergeant?" asked one of the lads.
"Yes, now, you silly b...r", was the reply.

Anyway, I liked the little pork pie hats and chin straps and the familiar look of some of the chargers – a thick white cord from under the horse's chin to his breast was much more becoming than the cart harness. Those meetings were part of the rural activities.

Next let us continue down the lane called Vicarage Lane, between the Vicarage and the Church. At the bottom facing you is Goldmine Farm. I have, years ago, seen an old newspaper cutting about gold being found on the land – probably that is how it got its name.

Turn left and at the end is South Bank, the home of Dr Peter Love. There are also three old cottages, in the middle one of which, years ago, lived Bessie and Ephraim Eyes. Bessie always kept a pig and it was the custom, when we boys were a little bored with our usual devilment, to go and look at Bessie's pig. Asked one night when she was going to have the pig killed, she replied,

"If I'm going to keep a pig, I may as well keep the old one".

This was a disappointment to us because at all the local killings we would wait until Mr Armstrong of Aston had killed, scalded and dressed the victim. When it was opened up we would be given the bladder. This would be blown up, tied to a stick or string and used to clout each other about the head. If two or three pigs were killed at a time, apart from the bestial screaming being doubly or trebly horrific, there were enough bladders for us to engage in a friendly affray.

Back now to the farm and keep straight on down the narrow lane. This is a public footpath through the fields and on to the main Northwich-Warrington road. The path is seldom used but is still a right of way. Facing you, over the main road, and shut off to the public is Mere Lane. In the old days almost everyone used this road down to the Mere – the younger people certainly did. We would go in the school holidays for whole afternoons, bathing and fishing – it seems to me we had weeks of glorious weather. What would perhaps seem strange today is that we boys would go without any bathing costume or towel – we would run round the field until we were dry. I remember too, we would run much faster if someone shouted

"Here's Johnny".

That would be Mr John Drinkwater, farmer and Licensee of the Cock Inn, who farmed the field we passed through and where our clothes were left on the grass by the water's edge. If he seemed to be heading our way we would gather our clothes and seek sanctuary across the brook that feeds the Mere from Pickmere. The field on the other side was tenanted by Mr Farish and was the spot where the Marston lads would come to bathe. If the Marston lads were there, they would eye us over and perhaps grant us temporary respite. They were a tough lot and seemed to me always to be looking for a scrap. They were always referred to as Marston Bulldogs, just as outsiders referred to us as Budworth Dusters. I know, as an apprentice at a Northwich builders I was always the 'duster'. How many villages had their nicknames? 'Anderton Blacks', 'Comberbach Swilltubs', 'Weaverham Russetts' and 'Norley Gorgers' are a few I remember.

The Holden Boys: Albert, John, Cecil and Arthur

Having mentioned John Drinkwater from the Cock, I would like to refer to the times when we boys were taken on Saturdays and holidays into the potato or hay field. It was entertainment for us to listen to Johnny and any of his workmen who engaged him in conversation. My boyhood friend Bill, in the village, will remember how devastating he could be. One day, and it was a beautiful day, we were in the hay field where Johnny had brought us baggin'. One of the workmen said,
"*I hope we get a fine spell of weather just now*". Johnny replied, "*I don't give a b...r if it snows, I can thatch my house in £5 notes*".

Only one man never seemed to be daunted – he lived in Crow Nest Lane, 'Old Ninety' or 'Ninter' - I can't remember which – a funny little man. Whenever anyone mentioned any place in England, Ninter had always lived or worked there. Adding the years he lived in these various places to the years we knew he had lived amongst us made him about 190 years old. As I said, he could hold his own with Johnny or anybody else. If half the things happened as told by Ninter, then some very strange things happened at that time.

I should mention the Mere itself. Budworth Mere, not Marbury Mere, is a lovely stretch of water approximately one mile in length covering about 80 acres.

It is now used by the Manchester Sailing Club and fishing can be arranged. Personally, I have never stopped going down and walking through 'the Cover' (covert).

Of course, I have, since the '20s, asked permission and have never been refused.

At the opposite end is Marbury Hall. This manor dates from as early as the reign of Henry III, the property and residence of the family of Merbury. The line ended in 1684 with the death of Richard Merbury esquire. It has since been the home of the Smith Barrys, an army depot and is now used by ICI to house some of their workers. I should say its end is not far off.

Now back to the Church and Vicarage. The vicar in my early days was Canon Holme, a portly, cheery man who used to drive around in a trap with a grey pony. He was one of the last of the old private income clergy. He was quite generous to us choir boys and choir practice was held in the vicarage with plenty of lemonade and cakes until he was hit in the face with one, injudiciously entering in the middle of a bun-fight. Any adult was announced by his housekeeper as, 'Such and such a choirboy's father', until one day a Mr Walter Holmes called. The Holmes family were blacksmiths, our homely housekeeper announced him as Wat Holmes, whereupon the Canon enquired, *"What Holmes?"* and they went on from there. In the end when they had sorted out 'what' was 'wat' the Canon asked Walter when he was going to start coming to Church.

Wat replied, *"When they pay me like they do thee"*.

Down School Lane, a stone cobbled road, there are some fine old half-timbered cottages on the left. In the last of the cottages lived, a long time ago, a man of whom it is said that, after having got a job as a railway porter at Lostock, he sat up all night shouting "Plumley for Tabley" whilst opening and slamming the oven door. The tale has it that he also had the cat in the oven as a passenger with near capital results.

Adjoining the cottage is the old Hearst House and, until recently, the village stone mason's workshop. Generations of Cockseys were masons and sextons of the church. I remember the last but one sexton at the church, Mr John Cocksey, he wore a bright red tunic when on duty at the church services and did seem to me then a very colourful person, his opposite number today we would find outside a cinema.

I was looking though some old churchwarden's accounts some time ago and came across the cost of this same coat, made by 'rayner' the village tailor. Now whether it was bright spots like this that attracted seven hundred people to some of the church services I can't say – this figure is quoted as at the Harvest Festival in a magazine in my possession. The wearing of this tunic was discontinued about 1910, when a black gown was substituted.

I noted also in the same accounts an item several times for the cleaning of the hearse and of the leads of the hearse. I think it must have been a much larger vehicle than the gun carriage bier we have today.

The hearse cart in High Street

Opposite the cottage and hearst house stands the old school, founded by Sir John Dean in 1600 AD, a fine old building, it has just undergone an extensive restoration to the fabric and should be a useful place for the village to have. Years ago it was a club and a reading room and is still, indeed, often referred to as the reading room to-day.

A few yards futher on and we come to the Parochial School and School House, or should I say what was the School House until a short time back The school was erected in 1857 AD together with a school house at a cost of £1,000 raised by public subscription and a grant from the government, it is now a junior school. The writer remembers well the old headmaster at the time that he was a schoolboy and many are the tales that could be told of him for he was of legendary calibre.

One day he was questioning one lad on the subject of nicknames, we nearly all had one. One boy he asked about did not, however, have one and the old man wished to know why. The lad he was questioning informed him *"Please Sir, he doesn't come out at night"*. Ever afterwards the headmaster referred to him as 'the boy who doesn't come out at night.'

Continuing past the school we will come to the Avenues, a lovely walk through under the lime trees until we come to the Knutsford Road. I should mention that half way along the second length, on the right hand side, there is, or should be, a stile, the entrance to a public footpath and right of way to Aston Hall Farm. This stands on the Aston-Marston Road and on old maps it is called Hield House.

I think that I should mention here an occasion which concerns some of the young men of the village. Many years ago, a certain young man from Arley was 'sweet' on one of the village girls and asked his workmate on the estate, a Budworth lad, if he could do anything about a meeting with the aforementioned lass. The Budworth lad said he thought he could arrange it and would tell him the next day. Well now, the Budworth boys got together and arranged that the girl's brother should dress up in his sister's clothes and meet the young man from Arley at the bottom of Farthing Lane, where it joins the Avenue, at a certain time on a particular night. The young man from Arley arrived and sure enough there was the girl, large hat and veil and fairly well disguised. Now the young man, no doubt wishing to make the most of this evening, started to show the girl how much he thought of her and fairly early on discovered that the girl was a little different from what he expected. The boy-girl also became a little alarmed and set up an unearthly scream, gathered up the long skirts that were worn then and moved towards the village in a hurry. I can't write here what the young man from Arley said but I do know he was chivvied about the affair for years.

Back in the centre of the village, opposite the Church, is a finely constructed Pump House. Adjoining, the first house in Church Street, we have the last of the old pubs, 'The Ring o' Bells', again a very old half-timbered house. It was for many years the main shop and Post Office. It is now kept, and has been for the past forty years, by Mr and Mrs F Hubbard. To all the children it is 'Hubbards'.

Years ago when it was the Post Office, the proprietress, Emma Platt, had not got the cat under proper control and, as the story goes, the more daring of the boys would ask for, "a pennyworth of them (toffees) that the cat's lying on".

Later Miss Platt married one 'Adam Boardman', a most go-ahead young man who caused quite a stir by contracting to run the Royal Mail from Northwich to Crewe. What a do it was for us to watch the bright red van being prepared and the harnessing up of the horses. It was also from this shop that the Northwich Guardian was distributed, the writer and other boys tried to be there just when they arrived so that they could take them from door to door around the village.

The spot just outside the shop was once the scene of a great legal argument. One day a young lady issued from one of the houses opposite with bucket and shovel to collect some horse muck lying in the road. She was prevented, however, by an equally determined young lady from an adjoining house. After some discussion the latter young lady opined that it couldn't be the first young lady's property and when asked why, she said, "*Our Dolly's done it*", which settled the argument. The first girl, not to be completely routed, replied, "*You'd better have it then*", and threw it all over the other lady's clean step.

Opposite the shop is an opening leading to what is called Corporation Yard, why no-one seems to know. When I was a young man it was called Birtles's Yard. Barney Birtles, for many years a widower, washed the floor every morning and sprinkled it with sand.

The tale goes about a certain young lady, who shall be nameless, that she was standing outside the house with a few neighbours one day, undoubtedly gossiping which, together with pimping and tooting, is as skillfully carried out in Budworth as anywhere else. They noticed some children coming out of a Bible class and her eyes falling, at a distance, upon a rather scrawny lad, she remarked, "*Whose that poor little b....?*" As she said it the group came into focus and she recognised 'her Frank'.

I was born in Church Street and played in the yard as a child. Maybe it was because the Birtles family used it as a dump that it carried their name.

I remember an old farm cart in the yard and there is still evidence of some kind of shippon on one of the boundary walls. There was also a little land to the place up the sand hole. This sand hole lies in the fields over the road from the far end of the Avenue and was the place where Arley estate took out sand for building purposes. It has since been used by Runcorn RDC as a tip for the dust carts.

The yard does, however, serve the cottages with a drying ground but why 'Corporation Yard' I can't imagine.

Just in the yard and on the corner of the first old cottage there was, years ago, a communal swill tub which was a stock pot for the pigs. Almost anything and everything was put in it. Occasionally us boys would give it a stir up and the stink was terrific – not even bluebottles would go near it for a time. Well, we had to do something, being boys. There was no Wells Fargo or Lone Ranger for us to run home to view – early arrival from school usually meant a longer session weeding in the garden.

The gabled house on the corner of School lane and Church Street, facing the George and Dragon, was the home many years ago of a queer little man named Maginty. He would run out in his stockinged feet to look at the Church clock and if it was too late for work his language was unprintable. On the right as you proceed along Church Street are four old world cottages, the last one of the four has been re-fronted. The rear portion is very old, half-timbered with a crook gable at the rear. This method of building with infilled panels was inexpensive and serviceable as all the materials were at hand – thick stakes, covered with reeds from the Mere were faced with a mixture of mud and cow dung, the whole was called 'wattle and daub'.

Opposite the writer's own house, formerly a farmhouse, the shippons front the street. It is dated on the front panel 1725, with the initials JHS, one of the Starkeys who built and owned a number of houses in the village. The Starkeys originated from Stretton, a very old family mentioned in the earliest books.

On the right, and next to the old cottages, is the tall gabled Providence House. Years ago this was a ladies' seminary and the schoolroom still remains at the back. Next door, and set back behind a well-kept garden is Providence Cottage. This was at one time part of the seminary, probably the staff quarters.

Nearly opposite stand three cottages. I remember, as a boy, there lived in the first a Miss or Mrs Towers. It was said she would not retire for the night until the cat came in so that she could hold it out and so sleep peacefully in the sure knowledge that there would be no little pools in the morning.

Opposite these stands a detached red brick house. This was the last of the four shops mentioned earlier. 'Cooks' the butchers and general stores. I remember as boys we would stand outside under the window and talk. Also, I remember bunches of 'dips' hanging from the ceiling – these, by the way, were thin candles.

Next to this we come to Cob Cottage. I should say this is one of the oldest houses in the village where once lived a very remarkable man named John Heath, known to all for miles around as John M'norkey. Why M'norkey no-one seems to know but probably he kept some Black Minorca hens, which were very popular at that time and M'norkey is a type of off-beat mispronunciation which Budworth people cultivate. He was a bricklayer on the then Arley estate and travelled to work in a donkey cart. One day on his way up the drive to Arley Hall he passed the Squire in a carriage. The Squire, not very pleased, questioned Heath about this and Heath replied, *"You mun keep better cattle"*.

He was a very good workman and was responsible for some of the artistic chimneys which are a feature of many of the houses in the village. Like many another character with a sharp turn of phrase, he found the local parson fair game – the vicar was asked if he would pray for him as he had a floating kidney. The cleric was both pleased and puzzled by this request and he complimented Heath on his faith but observed that it was a rather bizarre ailment. This was, of course, just what Heath was waiting for and he promptly informed his reverence that he regularly prayed for 'loose livers'.

Opposite Cob Cottage and the last house on the left-hand side of Church Street is the Old Smithy Cottage, the home time past of the old village blacksmith. The last smith in practice was quite a character, Charlie Blackstock, and anything less like 'the smith a mighty man is he' would be hard to find. One or two of us have often wondered whatever became of Charlie's diary. Surely it would make fascinating reading now, for Charlie kept a diary of all the village happenings and is said to have filled it in faithfully in detail every day.

Memories of Great Budworth ~ ~ Cecil Holden

John Holden, cabinet maker

Leave by the road now and continue down Smithy Lane and you will pass by the way a nice old cottage on the corner. Continue down the lane which is known more popularly as 'The Butts' probably because the old militia used to do their firing practice in the field at the bottom. On some old maps it is called 'Robin Hood's Butts' and it is not too much to suppose that it was used for archery practice in mediaeval times. The field at the bottom, just mentioned, is called Brick Hill field. The estate until, say, fifty years ago, took clay out to make bricks for estate work. I believe that bricks used in the building of Dene House were made of clay taken from this field. The holes that were left filled with water and are known as 'Brittle Pit'. I remember as children that we always tried the ice on these before venturing down to the Mere. First we would throw a large stone on the ice, then, very warily we would try it ourselves. If the ice was thick enough there would soon be a slide across.

Before we continue back to the entrance to the Butts, on the right is what was the old smithy, now the Parish Hall and used for various entertainments. I remember the open part of the building, which was called The Hovel. We would meet there as lads and practice our lines for Soul Caking night. The lighting we used for the souling was one or two hollowed-out turnips with a candle inside, 'Guinea Gongs'.

It was here also, at the smithy, that we had our trundle hoops and hooks made and repaired.

Nearby are three new houses – I suppose we cannot escape entirely from some new buildings.

Now carry on down the lane, over the stile, and you may walk through the fields along a right of way and a public footpath to Budworth Heath.

You will emerge on the highway, leading on the right to Aston-by-Budworth and on the left to Comberbach and Winnington. Facing you on this corner is the old school, built in 1845, by Mrs Leigh of Belmont Hall. Turn right and continue towards Aston, a hundred yards, and before you reach the crossroads there is a small circular patch of trees known as Quebec Wood. This was planted at the time of Woolf's great victory. Nearly everyone calls the larger wood Quebec but this is incorrect, it is Belmont Plantation.

Now turn right at the crossroads and continue towards the village, a pleasant walk for half a mile before you reach the three lane ends at the top of Farthings Lane.

You will find, if you look on the left-hand side just after passing the new farm, a gateway that gives access to a right of way to the Aston Road, emerging at Hilltop Farm.

Just to the left of the opening of Farthings Lane is an old half-timbered house and left again, towards Aston, there is, set back from the road, a very old farmhouse. I remember many years ago the old man, Mr Yearsley, who lived there. It was said that he could not read; he once picked up a weekly newspaper in the George and Dragon tap room, held it upside down and, on seeing an advertisement for a shipping line with a picture of a ship, remarked,

"I see there's been another shipwreck".

Once on the way to work at Arley he saw a notice on a building in the fields which said 'Stick No Bills'.

"Wat's it say?", asked Yearsley.

"Take no sticks", said Sam Worrall.

"Oh," said Yearsley, *"that Billy Miller's been telling tales again".*

Now towards the village you will pass the council estate and police house, all very pleasant and well kept.

By the way, this length of road is called Westage Lane, a harmless enough name, however, just as I prefer 'The Butts' to 'Smithy Lane', I prefer the older names for this stretch of road. When, and why, were the names altered? I know that what was then 'The Westage' was from the sandhole entrance to the three lane ends at Aston and this short length towards the village was called Maltkiln Lane or more popularly 'The Morkle'. That is how it is marked on my old map, surveyed in 1875, revised 1908 – the road is not west of the village. Probably the council did not know the old name when they fixed the road names a few years ago.

In the field opposite the houses the Wakes Fair was held. I remember, as a boy, Peter Brown would come each year until he seemed to be part of our Festival. He had the usual side shows and Hurdy Gurdy organ. This instrument had some defective pipes because a few were stuffed with paper. If there was no member of the Brown family near, we boys would smartly remove some of these paper plugs – the noise was indescribable. Local help was enrolled on the stalls and we would benefit if one of our friends or relations was in charge of the coconut stall.

I remember, too, old 'Alice Anne' whom we have met before, the housekeeper at Haughton's farm at the top of Cock Lane. I never knew her surname. She would come down with a lantern clipped on a belt around her waist and on arrival she would blow out the light and put the lantern round to her back. One of us lads would engage her in conversation whilst another of us crept up and re-lit the lamp. Eventually she would find the heat overbearing and we would have to make ourselves scarce. Where the lay-by is now, was once Sally Walker's pit but no-one seems to know why it bore that particular name.

Now we come to the last building on the left before rejoining Church Street. This building, hidden behind the trees, is the Wesleyan Church. Although the writer is Church of England I think the Wesleyans deserve a better site than this. However, it is still used and kept neat and tidy.

Back now along Church Street to the Church. It consists of a nave, chancel, side aisles and two transepts, with a fine tower and a peal of eight bells. The Church is dedicated to Saint Mary and All Saints, the dedication festival or 'Wakes' is celebrated on the first Sunday after 8th November. Ancient parish festivals generally had a religious beginning, very commonly the anniversary of the dedication of the parish church became the yearly festival. No doubt it was the same in our parish. All Saints' day is 1st November, the All Saints' festival, in its fullest sense, is from 1st November to 8th November. Naturally, therefore, our parish festival should fall in the first week in November. Why it is in the second week there is nothing to show; very likely the difference may be a relic of the reckoning of days by the old style. 'Give us back our eleven days.'

The Restoration, begun in 1955, is nearing completion and over £15,000 has been raised towards the £17,000 required. Opposite the West door in the churchyard may be seen kneeling stones, that is low head stones to graves, shaped for the knees to rest in. The Lychgate was erected in 1921 as a memorial to the fallen in the 1914-1918 war.

Outside, near the wall, are the stocks which were restored by voluntary effort in 1952. They were last used in the 1600s and are now scheduled by the Ministry of Works as an ancient monument. The old men of the village used to lean on them and talk but now children seem to have taken possession.

Before leaving the village, just a word about one or two happenings without being too specific as to the place. People always had to be very careful, for, one unguarded moment, and an unfortunate phrase was tied to a person for life. There was the poor little girl who came to the door and shouted up the street, *"Our Mary, come in for your half egg. If you don't come you'll be thrashed and if you do come you'll be thrashed, so you'd better come"*.

A certain man had several daughters, who, being in domestic service, cultivated a refined accent. The fellow was a great pigeon fancier and on being asked by one of his returning daughters, *"Have the birds come home father?"*, replied, *"Get on in th'ouse, wi' thee debroidery talk"*.

Again, the same fellow in the house, enquired one night, *"What the hell's burning?"* One of the girls replied *"T'aint our skirts father"*.

There was the affair of the old chap who was taken out and plied with small beer by a couple of the local boys; they had to assist him home in a merry state. The old man's housekeeper wasn't very pleased but she was a bit more subtle than most and refrained from making a frontal attack. The old lady was rather a dab hand with home-made wines and solicitously uncorked a special sample for the lads for being so kind as to bring the old man home. As they put it themselves, they are not too clear what happened after the fresh air hit them. However, after sitting scriking on a doorstep for a bit, one of them found his way home on hands and knees, guided by the other. The latter nearly frightened his wife to death by climbing into bed over the bottom rail – he said afterwards that he thought he was getting over a gate to go fishing.

Just a few words about 'Sandicroft', the large house about half a mile out of the village on the Comberbach road. The walk to this is a pleasant one with a good view of the Mere on the left.

It was, in the past, the Collegiate Institution. I quote from an old directory in my possession:

' ... built in 1852, expressly for educational purposes, is in the Elizabethan style and is excellently situated. It is fitted up with every possible convenience, and intended to afford the highest class of education. The masters, English and Foreign, are of high standing and of great experience, and are all resident. All that is necessary as regards health, food, exercise, and training of pupils, etc, is met with at 'Sandicroft', which can hardly, if at all, be surpassed by any similar institution in England. The pupils who have proceeded to the Universities and to the non-gremial examinations have all highly distinguished themselves. None but resident pupils are admitted.'

How long this institution continued in existence I cannot say, but I remember as a boy at the turn of the century, Mr George Egerton Warburton lived there. Many are the tales told of the different boys who were employed by him as stable boy, carriage attendant, etc. Mr George would visit the school periodically at school leaving time and cull himself a fine young specimen.

The Holden Girls: Maggie, Ettie and Annie

There was, for special occasions, when the lad accompanied Mrs Warburton to Arley etc, on the carriage, a special rig-out – tall shiner hat and long tail coat. These garments were almost adult size and much adjustment was necessary for the lads when newly left school. A Northwich Guardian or Chronicle, folded to the required thickness, usually did the trick for the hat, the thickness being reduced as the lad became older.

My friend, Hugh Hughes, from Antrobus, was the incumbent at one time and tells the tale of the time that he first accompanied the great lady. They got up the first slope as far as 'The Cock Inn', by which time the pony was blowing a bit. Mrs Warburton warned him that she might require him to get down and follow behind on foot up the next brew to Budworth Heath if the pony stopped trotting. Well, somehow there was a misunderstanding; Hughie got off more or less at the start of the 'bonk' and no sooner done than the lady put the hip to the pony. They soon began to put a bit of distance between themselves and Hugh, who had no alternative but to throw his long coat tails over one arm and hold his shiner on with the other and gallop after them. Round about Quebec Wood, the lady eased the pony to a walk and Hughie managed to climb aboard just as she said, *"I don't think there will be any need to get down, Hughes"*.

At a rather secluded spot in the back and behind of Aston-by-Budworth is a farm known as 'Gravestone Farm'. There is still remaining there, the gravestone of Jonathan and Sarah Vernon in the garden of the farm – they were buried here in 1692. Why they should have been interred in this spot I cannot say.

Well, just a word about how you may reach the village. Just near the Church is the bus stop for the service between Northwich and Great Budworth, running on Friday, Saturday and Sunday. The 'bus arrives at the half-hour and departs at a quarter to the hour.

A daily service between Warrington and Northwich passes the Pump House at the bottom of the Dene.

Should you chance to visit our village, I hope this small book will help you to recognise some of our old buildings. It is intriguing to think that some of the older people you may meet are descendants of the people who worked the land before the Domesday Book was written. In recent years many of them have regained the title deeds to their properties.

We are fortunate that the village is off the main road, and I hope that it will be a place worth visiting for many years to come.

Cecil Holden and his wife, Gwen, circa 1968

Harry Walton

The second collection of memories of Great Budworth were hand written in 1970s by Harry Walton. Unknown to him these were retyped and bound by his daughter Anne and her husband Robert Ellis, as a surprise for Harry's Golden Wedding in 1980. There were just five copies made, one copy was deposited at Northwich Library. The Editors are grateful to Anne and Robert for allowing this account to be included.

Harry's father moved to Great Budworth in 1901 from Northwich where he was a partner in a tailoring business Thompson and Walker. He took over the existing tailor's shop run by Thomas Raynor who had been the village tailor for most of the 19th Century. Harry senior was a well known character and served on the Great Budworth Parish Council and Runcorn Rural District Council and was a magistrate.

Harry junior was born and lived all of his life at 18 High Street, Great Budworth. In 1930 his father, Harry Walton senior moved to The Poplars, High Street. But the tailor's workshop remained at 18 High Street.

Like his father, Harry junior was the village tailor all his life. He was married to Sarah Heath and died in 1981. Anne was their only child.

The Editors

Harry Walton

HERE'S TO POSTERITY

With advancing years I find that the weeks appear to pass with increasing rapidity. One is inclined to view the past with a sense of nostalgia, and regrets the passing of many characters who provided so much colour and entertainment to village life in the days before radio and television.

In these pages I will endeavour to portray in small degree something of the atmosphere which pervaded village life in the early part of the century. All the anecdotes recorded here are, to the best of my knowledge, true. No effort has been made to change the names of the characters to whom I refer. I therefore request any surviving relatives to accept this narrative as a token of affectionate memory for the privilege of having known those concerned and as an appreciation of the colour, variety and entertainment their lives provided in an era which has now past.

Harry Walton

Chapter One ~ Setting the Scene

My late father came to reside in Great Budworth in 1902 and for well over half a century carried on the business as a country tailor employing a staff of five and sometimes as many as seven in the workshops at the rear of the premises. For twenty-seven years he represented Great Budworth on the Runcorn Rural District Council in an honorary capacity receiving no pay whatsoever. Today councillors are paid for their attendance at meetings.

I was born in the village in 1903 and still live in the same cottage, No 18 High Street. The atmosphere of the village and the way of life of its occupants have altered a great deal over the years and this narrative concerns chiefly the years of my childhood and adolescence.

Great Budworth being situated some three miles from a railway station, one had to either walk or cycle to the station, or go by pony and trap, in order to catch a train to either Manchester or Chester. Horse-drawn cabs awaited the arrival of passengers at Northwich.

Before the first world war very few people possessed a motor car. Farmers from miles around sent their milk by horse and float to catch the early milk trains to the city. Hay and straw were sent by rail and to ensure sufficient headroom under the bridges loads were measured by an arc device suspended on a gantry over the line. All country stations had their own sidings and local coal merchants received their stocks by loaded wagons. All heavy goods were transported by rail at this time and rolling stock was hauled by steam.

Despite modernisation, railway services are not in many cases as good as they used to be. For instance, Northwich then had a direct link with London Euston. I well remember a businessmen's train which ran from Manchester's Oxford Road station and which could be seen approaching Northwich around 11.20 am each morning, the coaches bearing the black and white livery of the old London and North Western Railway. This train, known as the White Lady, travelled along a single line to Crewe and then on to London Euston.

Early in 1931 my wife and I travelled to London leaving Northwich at 5.35 pm catching the London train at 6.05 from Crewe, arriving in London around 8.50 which was considered a very good time in those days.

I can recollect Greenall Whitley, the brewers from Warrington, had a fleet of steam wagons on the road, some of which could be seen drawing water from the stream which used to run along the side of the main road.

This stream has now been piped and filled in. These Sentinel steam wagons often had a trailer attached, laden with the wooden barrels which have now given way to metal containers.

I well remember local farmers going with horse and cart to Burford Lane coal wharf on the Bridgewater Canal near Lymm for coal, for which they paid sixpence per hundredweight. Cord trousers, fully lined, were 10 shillings and sixpence per pair. A three-piece suit, made-to-measure, hand-stitched and with the best trimmings, cost two pounds and ten shillings.

Woodbine cigarettes were five for one penny; Capstan and Goldflake sold at six pence for ten. Petrol was about one shilling and sixpence per gallon. Farm wages were about eighteen shillings per week and cottage rents were very low, in many cases being less than two shillings per week. Jim Hughes who followed his mother as tenant at 19 High Street, never paid Arley Estate more than two shillings and sixpence a week, for a detached house with three bedrooms and a large garden. He used to say that what he made from the sale of raspberries paid his rent. Farm rents were about two pounds to two pounds ten shillings per acre.

Practically all the villagers were employed locally. The main sources of employment were agriculture, Brunner Mond, Salt Union, gentlemen's service and Arley Estate. Great Budworth is now largely a dormitory for business people from the industrial belt of South Lancashire or Greater Manchester.

Small cottages in Budworth village which were sold by Arley Estate in 1948 at prices well below £200, are now selling at £16,000 to £20,000. Reorganisation of local government has in many cases resulted in more bureaucracy, diminution of services and higher rates.

Facilities prevailing in the village seventy years ago were somewhat primitive. Each cottage had a pail closet which was emptied into the garden or, in some cases, into a large hole called a bog hole which was usually emptied once a year. There was no refuse collection; old bottles, tins and cinders were piled in some corner at the back or in the garden, and were eventually taken away by horse and cart or in a wheelbarrow to be dumped into a convenient pit hole or taken to the sandhole, a tip now filled in, some little distance outside the village. Artificial light was provided by the old-fashioned oil lamp. Water was carried from five taps or conduits which were situated at various points in the village.

At the end of the last century there were three public houses in the village in addition to the Cock Inn and the George and Dragon. They were The Saracen's Head, The White Hart next to the vicarage and the Ring o' Bells at the corner of Church Street. They all brewed their own ales. The Ring o' Bells has been a Post Office, a village shop and now is a private house.

Aviation was then in its infancy and very few aircraft were to be seen. The absence of cars from the village streets rendered it completely safe for children to run along the road trundling their hoops, or play in the centre of the street with their spinning tops and whips.

Village life at the time of which I write was lived at a more leisurely pace, people were more content and there was a much stronger sense of belonging to a community where everyone knew each other. Practical jokers there were, but they were without malice.

The Walton Staff, circa 1908

Centre of back row: Harold Heyes, who came to work in Budworth in 1901 and continued to work for Mr Walton for 51 years, most of that time cycling from Northwich each day, regardless of the weather.
End right, back row: Harry Walton senior
End right, front row: William Walton, Harry Walton senior's father
Centre front: Harry Walton junior

Chapter Two ~~ Church Traditions

Great Budworth church has a peal of eight bells which, unfortunately are now seldom rung, and it is dedicated to Saint Mary and All Saints. The patronal festival or wakes is always celebrated on the first Sunday following the 8th of November. In the early years of this century wakes week saw the arrival of Peter Brown's fair and I have a vague recollection of my father accompanying me to the fair ground on what was their last visit. I can dimly recall the naphtha flares and the blare of the roundabouts and the general sense of excitement.

For many years there was a wakes dance held in the school but this has not been held for some time now. Apart from the church services, the wakes is now commemorated by the annual social and hot pot supper.

The highlight of the wakes social used to be the song rendered by the late John Lever, entitled 'The Red Light'. I can still remember part of the refrain :- 'Green light shines bright go ahead with caution, but when we see the red we know there's danger on the line'.

I was told that in the last century Budworth wakes was an even greater occasion and that races were run from the bottom of the hill to the church gates. The late Thomas Owen of Crowley Lodge used to speak of the time when, as a boy, he attended Budworth pig fair. Pigs were offered for sale and exhibited in crates placed down the side of the village street.

This Thomas Owen took his wife to Northwich one market day in his horse and trap. Whilst in town his wife, who was heavily pregnant, went into labour and Thomas realised it was too late to make the journey back home. His youngest son was born in the Crown and Anchor Hotel and was named Wallace, the name of the licensee.

I distinctly remember the old canon, Arthur Phideas Holme, driving through the village with his high trap and grey mare. Any child who failed to touch his cap to the old canon was likely to get a flick from his horse whip.

Amongst the old customs no longer observed was the ringing of the curfew bell which was rung with unfailing regularity from October to March at eight pm and was followed by the date bell - one ring for each day of the month. On the eve of a funeral a passing bell was rung and this was concluded by ringing down the scale on each bell, three strokes for a male and two strokes for a female. Each Sunday at one pm a bell was rung to announce evensong and sermon at six thirty pm.

37

Many years ago years ago I was waiting in a bus queue at the Northwich terminus and standing next to me was my next door neighbour Mrs. Moores (May Dickens), whose father had been captain of the Great Budworth bell ringers for many years during his lifetime. It was a Tuesday and Witton Church bell ringers were holding their customary evening practice. I remarked to May how nice it was to hear them. *"Yes,"* she replied, *"if my father came back now wouldn't he think it funny hearing Budworth bells silent?"*

Chapter Three ~~ Our Market Town

I well remember as a small child walking across the fields to Northwich with my mother - she died when I was a boy of eight. Northwich nearly seventy-five years ago was a very different place from the Northwich we know today. Much of the property at that time stood at a precarious angle with the windows and doors all awry. Many shops had subsided to such an extent that doors and windows were partially below street level. It is said that travellers who came to the town once or twice a year never knew whether they would have to go up stairs or down them into a shop.

I particularly remember my father's stepmother had a bed sitting room at a Mrs Gallimore's, a house on Winnington Hill near to the entrance to Verdin Park and when you opened the door the floor sloped at an angle so acute that there was a danger of sliding across the room and disappearing under the bed which was supported by the outside wall.

At the Witch and Devil public house which stood near the junction of the Old Warrington Road and Marbury Lane conditions were so bad that the occupants had to cross the yard to the outhouses in a rowing boat. This pub and a row of houses eventually disappeared overnight. Today practically all the buildings in Northwich are constructed on a timber or steel girder framework which can be jacked up if the foundations give way. There is, however, very little subsidence caused by the pumping at the present time. The introduction of controlled pumping in the 1930s has virtually solved the problem.

I can remember when the canal burst its banks at Marbury in July 1907. Much could be written about Northwich and its past industries, many of which are now gone. It is no longer possible to walk to Northwich across the fields - subsidence in Forge Lane and later demolition of the canal bridge brought this pleasant walk to a close.

Again, many of the familiar landmarks along the road have disappeared, Marston Church and school, the Adelaide rock mine and Ashton's salt works to name but a few. I could name between twenty and thirty public houses which have either closed or been demolished over the last half century between Northwich station and the Bull Ring. We are, however, considering Great Budworth and I will endeavour to confine my efforts with this object in view.

Chapter Four ~~ The Outskirts of the Parish

The civil parish of Great Budworth is in itself somewhat small, whilst the ecclesiastical parish covers a wide area embracing Marbury, Comberbach, Marston, part of Wincham, Aston-by-Budworth, Pickmere, part of Tabley, Arley and Crowley. The west of the civil parish is bounded by a brook which runs under the A559 just beyond Belmont Hall, crossing Crow Nest Lane and the road to Comberbach at Kidbrook.

Albert Johnson succeeded his father in business here at Kidbrook and, for many years, was well-known as a joiner, wheelwright and undertaker. He was a very unassuming chap but I always remember a remark he passed on the occasion I attended a Methodist funeral with him at Knutsford. *"I do enjoy a good chapel funeral,"* said Albert with great sincerity, *"every bugger sings".*

A little way along the road Randal Beresford Slacke was in residence at Boxhedge, a detached house standing in its own grounds. Sandicroft, a big rambling house which had at one time been a boys' school known as Stedman's College, was occupied by George Egerton Warburton, agent to Arley Estate. George Warburton had at least two maids and a liveried coachman (Frank Hubbard) who wore a silk hat with a cockade at the side. My father once made a white piqué costume for Mrs Warburton to use for gardening. Brownslow was occupied by Dr Thomas Windsor.

Peter Scott lived at the bottom of Budworth Hill opposite the running pump. Peter's garden was well known for the colourful display of dahlias, which he grew each year, and it is said that he used some very strong expletives when the village boys had great fun flicking pieces of slate across the top of his dahlias in an endeavour to cut most of the flower heads off.

The first of the two cottages on Warrington Road which bear the inscription:- Take thy calling thankfullie, Love thy neighbour neighbourlie, Shun the road to beggarie', was lived in by the Walker family. Joe, Elsie and Harry were the first wife's family and the father was employed as butler at the Dene House.

Once the dowager house to Arley Estate, the Dene stands down a drive on the right of the A559 - going in the direction of Warrington - and was occupied by Mrs Ussher, who kept a staff of eight or more in regular employment: Walker the butler, Percy Staples and George Clarke footmen, Walter Jones coachman and later chauffeur, J Hart gardener, and Mrs Hassel, housekeeper. There were also two maids and Mrs Ussher had a companion referred to as Mademoiselle. She was often seen walking out two pomeranian dogs, a black one called Togo and a white one called Queenie.

Walter Jones, the coachman, had one daughter Amy, who will be remembered for her rendering at a wakes social of a song which had a refrain: 'Soldier, sailor, tinker, tailor - that's how the plum stones go'. John Drinkwater was licensee at the Cock Inn and his niece Ann Jane Kinsey kept house for him and later succeeded him as licensee.

The Brunners were then at Belmont Hall which was leased from the Moseley-Leigh family. Much could be written about Roscoe Brunner and his wife who was from Irish extraction, being the daughter of an Irish KC named Houston. Mrs Brunner was very impulsive both saying and doing things which she afterwards regretted. It will be remembered that the daughter Sheila married a Prince Andreas something or other of Liechtenstein.

Harry Walton and staff, 1946

**Left to right: Alice Pickering, Harry Walton junior, Harold Heyes, Hilda Griffiths, Edith Hammon.
Front row: Harry's daughter, Anne**

Alice Pickering worked for the Waltons from 1929 to 1973.

Chapter Five ~~ Belmont

The Brunners' lease of Belmont Hall expired about 1925. It was found that, in some of her more generous and expansive moods, Mrs Brunner had given away items which belonged to the Leigh family. Following an inventory, a four-figure sum was paid to Colonel Moseley-Leigh to compensate for missing goods and items of furniture. Domestic relations between husband and wife were somewhat strained, so much so that each had their own butler. Matters were probably accelerated by a court case in which Roscoe Brunner, as chairman of the then Brunner Mond and Co., accepted full responsibility.

This incident happened shortly before the formation of ICI in December 1926. Briefly, this is the story:- Lever Brothers Limited took over a firm then known as The New Pin Soap Company Limited. The old Brunner Mond Company was under contract to Lever Brothers to supply them with soda ash at a lower price than to their competitors. On gaining access to the books, it was ultimately discovered that the New Pin had been supplied by Brunner Mond at a lower price than Levers and, consequently, the Brunner Mond Company had to pay about one and a half million pounds in compensation. When ICI was established in December 1926, Roscoe Brunner's name was not included in the list of directors.

By this time the family had vacated Belmont Hall and taken up residence in Roehampton. It has been said that Mrs Brunner had been giving interviews to the press unknown to her husband. However, the climax came when both their lives were tragically ended in a shooting incident which occurred at their new home.

John James Davenport was the blacksmith at Belmont Smithy and he also sold bicycles. My father bought my first bicycle from there - a little green one of which I was very proud. There were three Davenport children, Frank, Nancy and Hilda. As a child going to Budworth School, I used to give Nancy Davenport my comic every week after I had read it. I always enjoyed the 'Chips' and characters such as Weary Willie, Tired Tim, Homeless Hector and Puss bring back memories of bygone days. The Davenports left the district sometime about 1912 and I understand that Mr Davenport became licensee of a pub near Birkenhead.

Widow Jones, her son Jim and two daughters Lizzie and Annie lived at the old one-story thatched cottage - on the left in Belmont Road. This cottage has now been demolished and a big modern house stands on the site.

A little further up the lane was the Home Farm, occupied by Samuel Dean. This was a thatched homestead and was destroyed by fire in 1912. What is now the Old School House was then a derelict building and was always referred to as The Mothers' Meeting House.

The Old School House, Budworth Heath

Tom Curbishley lived at Budworth Heath. He was a woodman on Belmont Estate and frequently used to walk to work at Latchford, a distance of several miles, where the estate had several acres of land which lay between The Manchester Ship Canal and The Mersey.

Passing Belmont Dairy Farm - then occupied by John McIntyre - we come to two cottages on the right known as Brook Cottages. Actually these cottages are just outside the civil parish and are really the first cottages in Antrobus. My paternal grandfather from Northwich came to live in the first of these when I was little more than a toddler. He was a great admirer of David Lloyd-George and a staunch Liberal. Next door lived Mr Buckley, a roadman, whom my grandfather called 'an ignorant old bugger'. It appears that in the course of conversation grandfather mentioned Lloyd-George and Mr Buckley, evidently confusing Lloyd-George with Lord John Sangers, said that it was time the old bugger got back to his circus. (Lord John Sangers had a travelling circus at that time.)

Mr Buckley had a son who was also a character. He was an authority on beekeeping and it was his ambition to take honey by the ton, but he never did. He once said, *"I'll have a million working for me - but they'll all be bees."*

Coming back towards Budworth Village, the cottage on the right by the crossroads at Budworth Heath was called Mushroom Cottage. It was occupied by a family named Gibbon. It was aptly named as it was indeed shaped like a mushroom. The roof was thatched, and there was a portico around the outside supported by wooden pillars. This was also burnt down when I was about eight or nine years old and was completely rebuilt; it was renamed 'Wayside' and has now been completely modernised.

The cottage on the left of the crossroads was then thatched and occupied by a family called Withenshaw. I mention the Withenshaws largely because members of the family attended Budworth Wesleyan Chapel when both my parents were Sunday School teachers. Mr Withenshaw was employed for many years by George Priestner at Heath Farm. There were two sons, Dennis and Joe who was a dwarf, and two or three girls. On occasion they would take the local preacher home to tea on a Sunday following afternoon service.

Another dwarf-like figure who lived at Budworth Heath at that time was Bill Jackson, better known as 'Giant'. He worked for local farmers and always had a keen sense of humour and a bright and cheerful disposition.

Michael Platt lived at White House – now enlarged and modernised. He lived as a recluse and was none to particular about cleanliness. I understand his sister Emma married Adam Boardman and was the postmistress in Budworth village.

The Post Office was then round the corner past the George and Dragon and, later, became Hubbard's shop. Tom Littler, his wife and family, had a little shop in a thatched cottage just down Budworth Heath Lane. An old pump and garden hedges confirmed the fact that there had been other cottages on this site at some time previously. A little further down the lane lived the Bakers with a family of fifteen children.

Chapter Six ~~ The Village Folk

As we have now dealt with some of the families on the perimeter of the village, we will return to the foot of the hill and pursue our way up the main street of the village itself. On the left at the top of the hill was the home of the Birtles family. Billy Birtles, as he was known, caused something of a sensation when he married Nurse Fletcher. Although they never lived together, the nurse made an excellent stepmother to the three children May, Elsie and Sidney.

The village is unique in that the cottages are all numbered consecutively round the village.

At this time there were five Scott, five Hughes and four Dickens families in the village, which could have led to a great deal of confusion but of course the natives had their own ways of distinguishing one from another in conversation. The Scotts were identified as Fat Jim, Thin Jim, Jack, Old Peter, and Old Mrs Scott who lived in School Lane.

John Lever occupied the cottage at the far end of The Mount. He was for many years a chorister in the church choir, and is reputed to have replied to a remark on the inclement weather made by the old Canon Holme, *"Yes Sir, we have had a lot of shite lightening lately."* The worthy canon's reaction is not known. John's wife Sarah said at a sewing class, *"I can't see where I'm stitching, but I'm getting on."*

William Curbishley was next door at No 8. He was a joiner and wheelwright and had two nicknames; sometimes he was referred to as Moody, but perhaps he was better known as Flomp on account of the fact that he was very flatfooted. He was a man who had a fiery temper, and I have seen him chasing his two eldest sons up the village street brandishing an axe. His wife once went to Northwich and bought herself a dolly tub which she carried home herself across the fields - quite a feat!

Next we come to the Mellors. Mr Mellor was an ex-policeman and there was one daughter Annie. Mrs Mellor always told Annie that, when she went out with a young man, no harm would befall her as long as kept on walking. Annie must have taken her mother's advice to heart for she had become a staid middle-aged spinster often referred to as 'Hallelujah Merrylegs'. It was facetiously said that she wore her hat on three hairs.

Chapter Seven ~~ Jim Hughes

Jim Hughes lived at No 6. He was a remarkable character and a firm believer in ghosts, many of which he claimed to have seen locally. There is a true story concerning Jim Hughes who used to spend some time doing odd jobs for James Newhall, a painter and decorator who lived at the Old Hall in High Street.

Newhall had a field behind his house where he kept one or two cows and, having one of them near calving, he asked Jim to keep an eye on her that night.

One of Newhall's sons, knowing Jim's fear of ghosts, lay in wait carrying a white sheet suspended from a hayrake which he held up above the field gate as Jim approached in the early hours of darkness. Jim fled in terror - not surprising since, as Newhall's son stood some six feet tall, the supposed apparition appeared to be some eight or nine feet high. Jim retired to the George and Dragon where he had a few pints to give him courage. Alas! On his return to the field the apparition was still there and again he fled. Tom Astles, a brick setter from Arley, was coming down the street and was somewhat inebriated. Tom asked Jim what the matter was and, upon being told that there was a ghost some eight feet tall up the entry, Tom had to go and see for himself. He too ran back down the entry so fast that he was unable to avoid a collision with the front of the Saracen's Head farmhouse opposite. The two caused such a commotion that James Newhall came to investigate and comment on the smell. Drink, fear, and excitement had worked on Tom Astles more effectively than a good dose of salts.

Many more stories could be told concerning Jim. On one occasion he bought a billy goat for Mary Costello in Wincham. Mary's daughter was expecting a baby and she was afraid that a fright by the goat could result in the child being born with a beard. Jim was prevailed upon to take the goat off her hands and he could tell a very amusing story of his experiences in driving the animal home. On reaching the village, it got out of control completely and ran through the George and Dragon causing great consternation among the patrons.

Amongst his various accomplishments, Jim claimed to be able to grow hair on bald heads and charm toothache. He said that one night when visiting the George and Dragon he found Mrs. Bell, the licensee at that time, crying with toothache. He made one or two passes across her cheek with his hand.

"Oh! Oh! It's gone," exclaimed Mrs. Bell.

"Aye," said Jim, *"I've got it in my hand!"*

Jim Hughes' wife had been very ill and the late Dr G.L.Love had said she would not get better. Jim leaned over the bed and said, *"What am I going to do with these children when you are gone"*. To which his wife replied, *"Don't worry I am going to get better."* which she did.

He used to tell of an incident which he claimed actually happened during his wife's illness. One day as he lay on the settee, footsteps could be heard approaching and he said the settee creaked and he had the feeling of some unseen person lying beside him and a voice which said, *"I've come to cheer you up"*. After a short while the invisible form arose and he heard the footsteps receding. During this time he said the funny thing was that the coal shovel was shovelling coal in the coalhouse for all it was worth.

Jim once said that he had recourse to pay a visit to the lavatory, one dark night, and actually sat on a man who was apparently sleeping rough. Following a prolonged period of wet weather, Jim told of a pilot who flew his aeroplane through a cloud and, as he emerged on the other side he came across a fellow fishing.

The late Doctor Love had a dog that had died and which he had stuffed. Having told Jim he had a dog which he would like to train, the doctor derived considerable amusement and had great difficulty in controlling his hilarity as Jim endeavoured to coax the dog to come to him. Once Jim was sent to George Tomkinson - gamekeeper from Arley Estate - to bring a puppy home which he was to train. The animal was so thin that Jim claimed he had to blow its sides apart with a bicycle pump before he could bring it home.

Chapter Eight - More about High Street

The Bramhalls were at No 4 The Mount. I just about remember the old gentleman's death. Mrs Bramhall lived to a great age and could often be seen in the village street wearing her black cloak and bonnet and walking with the aid of a stick. Following the death of her husband, she made her home with her daughter, Mrs Craig, the dressmaker, who lived at 55 High Street. Another of Mrs Bramhall's daughters, Mrs Eaton, followed at 4 The Mount.

There was a son William who was a widower and was better known as Sossy Bramhall. His nickname is said to have derived from someone having remarked that they had sausages to which William replied, *"I like sossies"*- and he was known as Sossy ever after. He became a nomad sleeping rough and doing casual jobs to get a few pence to spend on drink. He often wore an old morning coat and a hard hat, and many times he slept in Mrs Craig's lavatory. If there was a wedding at church, Sossy was always at the lych gate to rope the newly-weds as they came out of church. (I don't know how widespread this custom is these days, but it still goes on in Budworth. When the newly-weds come out of church, their path is barred by a rope, and the bridegroom is expected to give a few coppers to those holding the rope before he is allowed to pass.)

Jim Hughes' youngest son Albert was very pally with Robert Curbishley (Flomp's son), and they were at one time quite inseparable. These two boys had been calling after Sossy and when the old man gave chase they ran up the left at Saracen's Head Farm, then the home of Joseph Porter. Robert Curbishley, seeing the old man following them, was so afraid that he jumped out of the pitch-hole on the cobbled yard below, but Albert, on seeing the old man ascend the ladder to the left, emptied half a hamper of rotten potatoes over him.

Albert Hughes was regarded as being the naughty boy of the village and if anything went wrong he always got the blame. On one occasion someone had cut off a cow's tail in a field up Budworth Heath Lane and Albert was said to be the culprit. It was consequently proved that at the time the incident occurred, Albert was absent from school but he had gone to a sale at Middlewich with Joe Porter. Mr Porter had to go to school to prove Albert's alibi.

Thomas Newton and his wife were at 'The Poplars' 53, High Street. Mr Newton was a cripple having a short leg. It was said that as a child he had fallen off a table at Arley Dairy Farm and sustained an injury which led to his disability. He walked with the aid of a crutch and kept a pony and tub which he drove to and from work each day. Parr's Bank in Northwich, where he was employed, stood on the right hand side of the road on the near bank of the river by Dane Bridge looking from the Bull Ring towards London Road.

Once when Mr Newton's pony and trap required some repair, he asked Joe Porter if he could provide him with transport to the bank; Mr Porter in turn asked Albert Hughes if he would drive Thomas Newton to Northwich. At that time there was a raised kerb with a piece of rounded sandstone twelve to fifteen inches high at each end on either side of the entrance to the pump house on the left hand side of the junction at the bottom of the hill. Albert got the pony going at too fast a pace down the hill, and, turning to the left at the bottom, he cut the corner so close that the wheel of the trap ran over one of the large stones.

Needless to say, Mr Newton was precipitated on to the floor of the trap, and as the rest of the journey was accomplished in hair-raising fashion he was a nervous wreck by the time he arrived in Northwich.

Mrs Newton was a Sunday School teacher at the Parish Church. She was a big woman and reputed to wear a bustle. A view from the rear and the way her posterior protruded added weight to this supposition.

Lizzie Hughes kept a catering establishment at 12 High Street. There was a sign outside, hanging over the front door, in the form of a bicycle wheel which was the insignia of the Cyclists' Touring Club. From time to time she had people staying.

Jim Hughes, whom we have already mentioned kept a pig which he fattened in a sty at his mother's, No 19 High Street. When the pig was ready to be killed, it was driven down the street to Jim's home in The Mount and Lizzie, Jim's sister-in-law, would walk in front of the procession ringing a bell, thus she acquired the nickname 'Blartin Liz'. She was a big-hearted woman but somewhat impulsive. The majority of the villagers were staunch Conservatives and I remember, on the occasion of one general election, Lizzie caught hold of my father who was a Liberal and rolled him in the snow.

Sam Worrall was at 'Mere View' No 14 High Street and was a joiner and undertaker. His wife also catered and provided teas for visitors. Sam was a craftsman of the old school and built a summer house at the bottom of his garden. It was surmounted with a weather vane in the form of dogs chasing a fox, and round the top of the outside wall was inscribed 'Waste Not Want Not.' Sam's summer house was quite a talking point, and the Squire having heard about it called to see it for himself. He admired it and remarked on the aptness of the inscription saying, *"Very nice, I notice you've used all my wood."*

Alfred Earl lived opposite and he and his wife once went to Blackpool with Ernest Southern and his wife - Lily Craig. While there they decided to pay a visit to the cinema. Never having been to the cinema before they were unaware that the seats tipped up and, having been shown to their seats by the usherette, they perched their rear ends on the edge of the seats much to the annoyance of those behind who immediately shouted, *"Sit down, we can't see."* Alfred unaware of the cause of the trouble turned round and said, *"Ee, we can see grand."*

The Duncalfs followed the Earls. William Duncalf, the father, was Joseph Porter's stepson. There were four boys and two girls none of whom lived to be very old. The eldest son Tom was about my age and he usually kept ferrets with which he occasionally went out rabbitting at night. I have heard him say the best night he remembered was when a hundred and thirty-five rabbits were netted on Northwood Farm at High Legh.

As a boy Tom was once thrashing his brother Fred. Mrs Holden opened her front window to see what was making so much noise. *"What are you hitting him like that for?"* she asked Tom. *"Can't you hear the young bugger how he's swearing?"* came the reply.

Tom lost the ends of several of his fingers as a boy when playing with a chop cutter at the Saracen's Head Farm, but I have seen him scratch out a rabbit from its burrow without a spade.

William Duncalf, who was influenced by his stepfather, liked a drink and once when he came home drunk, his wife Susan followed him to the lavatory and threw a bucket of water over him as he sat there to sober him up.

Peter Montieth Adair was a painter and decorator and his wife kept a shop at No 15 where she sold bread and a few sweets. Peter was a remarkable old man and he lived to be well over ninety years old. He used to tell a story that as a boy he was sent to deliver a parcel to some old quaker who asked if he would like a drink.

"*I don't mind,*" replied Peter.

After a good half hour or so the quaker returned

"*Why are you waiting there?*" he asked.

"Well," said Peter, "*you asked me if I would like a drink.*"

"*You said you didn't mind,*" the quaker replied, "*And I'm sure I don't.*"

At the age of 84, Peter Adair gilded the weather vane on top of the village church. His youngest daughter Eliza, better known as Cissie, had been badly burned as a girl but, despite the scar on her chin, she was a very attractive young woman. Her father was very strict and would not permit her to go dancing. There was, however, a convenient lean-to built directly under Cissie's bedroom window. She used to climb through the window and scramble down the roof where some amorous young man would be waiting to help her down and later help her return via the same route.

Mr. Adair had been married twice and his eldest son Sam, who was a regular soldier, married a German lady of uncertain age known as Dorothy Adair. After Sam's death the widow followed Mrs Dale as housekeeper at the vicarage for a time and later went to keep house for Bargy Bowden, who lived at the old smithy house at the far end of Church Street. Bargy Bowden was a widower and had a grown up family, but he had a burning desire to gain admission to Dorothy's bedroom. As he was not making much progress in that direction, to achieve his objective he caught a bat which he turned out in her room. On retiring to her bedroom that night, Dorothy was greatly alarmed to find a bat flitting about the room and called for Bargy to come to catch it and so his strategy succeeded.

49

I can just recollect the time when the present Post Office was a private house and an old couple lived there. Charlie Blackstock was a village blacksmith and moved into what is now the Post Office about 1907 or 1908. He had one son, Jim. It is said that when striking in the smithy Charlie used to say to his son *"Strike Jim! Strike with all your might but mind my bloody fingers."*

Mrs Blackstock occasionally used to strike the iron on the anvil. Charlie divided his Sunday worship between the parish church and the Wesleyan Chapel being what they called 'a brocken-haired un'. He was once asked to present the prizes at the chapel and it was customary to call the name of the recipient and then the title of the book.

"Jim Collins, Mother's Leg," called out Charlie, *"Nay, Nay, Mothers Legacy, aye that's it!"*

Harry Dickens at 17 High Street had one son, Harry. Young Harry used to go getting potatoes for local farmers for which he was paid twopence ha'penny for twenty yards up four drills. One of Harry's favourite expressions, when talking of someone, was to refer to them as a 'broken down old Tory' irrespective of their politics. I like the story concerning Matthew Moores who married Harry's sister, May. One night he came home in the bus, and, going to the George and Dragon, he found that there was a power cut and the place was lit by candles. Matt said, *"I can't understand it, I've just got off the bus and there were lights on the bus!"*

As previously mentioned, Joseph Porter was an occupant of Saracen's Head Farm and he was quite a character. Despite his having at one time been a local preacher, he was attracted by the ladies and he certainly liked a drink. This was about the time when Dr Crippen murdered his wife and absconded to America with Miss Le Neve in the guise of a young man. After James Newhall moved from the Old Hall, the property was let to a widow named Mrs Henshall who had a sister. Joe Porter used to visit this sister and he was nicknamed as Dr Crippen and Mrs Henshall's sister as Miss Le Neve.

Mr Porter and his stepson Billy Duncalf often went to market with the horse and cart. The horse would bring them home without any guidance and Mrs Porter would take the horse out of the shafts tipping up the cart and catapulting its two inebriated occupants on to the cobblestone yard, where they would remain until they sobered up.

Mrs Henshall had three children, a boy and two girls, and they could often be heard squealing as their mother chased them round the yard with a horse whip. The Henshalls were eventually evicted after numerous visits by the bailiffs. On one occasion she chased the bailiffs down the entry with a pikel (pitch fork), and on another occasion she lay in bed having covered herself with pins, their points upwards, so that she resembled a human hedgehog.

Chapter Nine ~~ Church Street and Southbank

Providence House, circa 1970

Providence House and Providence Cottage are next door to each other in Church Street and were once a girls' school called Miss Willett's Academy. I actually knew an old lady, a Mrs. Gibbon of High Legh, who attended this school when a girl. Jacksons were in residence at Providence House at the time of which I write and they too had a sign of the Cyclists' Touring Club displayed by their front door. Apart from catering, they often had one or two more school teachers boarded with them.

The Shinglers came later and they too let rooms. I well remember a district nurse who stayed there. She had a niece whose name was Mona Graves and who taught at the school for a time. This was after Nurse Birtles had left the village and would be round about the end of the first world war. At that time the local farmers used to hold an annual dance in the village school, often referred to as the farmers' ball. One Sunday, when having tea at Providence House, Mona Graves turned to me and said, *"Have you heard of any farmers' balls coming off lately, Harry?"* And then she wondered why everyone laughed !

Reverting back to childhood days, I remember Emma Boardman keeping the Post Office at the end of Church Street. Her husband, Adam, was considerably younger than Emma and it is said that he grew his beard to make himself look more her age. There was an Irishman named Sherry who I believe slept in the building at the back, and who used to carry Emma's liquid refreshment from the George and Dragon. What else he did I never knew.

Others worthy of mention include William Wright, one time licensee of the George and Dragon, Dr. Gilbert Love of the Manor House and Arthur Cook - shopkeeper and cab proprietor.

John and Charles Drinkwater, two bachelor brothers, were at Gold Mine Farm behind the church. John was tall and thin, whilst Charlie was shorter and fairly stout. Charlie was often referred to as Smiling Morn, probably because he seldom smiled. The Drinkwater brothers were often spoken of as the Potato Kings as they were usually first in the early potato market.

Philip Mules was tenant at Southbank - a detached house bordered on two sides by the churchyard, and another well-known character at that time was Jack Williamson. He was employed as coachman to old Canon Holme and later was gardener and general factotum with the Reverend FL Smithett who followed the canon as vicar.

Many years ago Mrs Williamson pushed me from one end of Marbury Mere to the other on a chair. This was one winter when the mere was frozen over, well before the first world war. On such occasions many of the villagers would go skating on the Mere.

Chapter Ten ~~ Visitors

For many years there was an old man named Carter, who walked from Warrington every Saturday night pushing a pram in which he carried weekly magazines and children's comic papers such as 'Chips,' 'Butterfly,' 'Lots of Fun' and 'Rainbow.' I recollect a women's magazine called 'Our Home' which was very popular at the time. Underneath his papers Carter would have a few boxes of chocolate cream bars tucked away in the bottom of his pram. He wore an old overcoat and a hard hat and, no matter what kind of weather it was, he never failed to turn up.

Jonathan Spencer used to live at Marston but he used to walk to Budworth Church to attend evening service every Sunday. He had a strong resonant voice but the trouble was he always sang at least half a line behind everyone else. He used to say that he could *"fair make them pews tremble"*. Old John Nixon, who was the retired schoolmaster, used to sit behind Jonathan encouraging him. *"Let it go Jonathan, let it go,"* he would say.

Tip Hewitt was another character. He had a sister, Mrs. Atkinson, who lived at Aston-by-Budworth, but as far as I know he lived rough. Tip was often the worse for drink and he once told Dick Cocksey, the sexton, that when he died he wanted inscribed on his tombstone :-

'Here lies Tip Hewitt,
Give him a drink, why,
Because when he was living,
He was always dry.'

Chapter Eleven ~~ School Days

I attended the village school until I was ten years old. When I first went to school the buildings were entirely different from what they are now. I think it would be about 1909 or 1910 that the school was largely rebuilt and the new classroom added at the back. The children were given a long holiday - seven or eight weeks - while the work was in progress. Bert Sproston was appointed headmaster following John Nixon who retired. After a stay of some four or five years Bert Sproston left to become headmaster of Victoria Road Council School in Northwich, and was succeeded at Budworth by Harry Smith who was a very keen disciplinarian and of whom I was frightened to death.

On his first day as headmaster this Harry Smith accused me of talking whilst lining up to go inside. Picking me up by the collar and the seat of my pants, he threw me down the step into school.

I remember Harry Smith asking Ernest Drinkwater when his birthday was. Ernest stood and regarded him with open mouth.

"Come come," said Mr Smith *"Surely you know when you were born!"*

"On a Saturday, Sir," replied Ernest

"Drinkwater, you are the limit! What did you say you were?"

"Please Sir, a linnet," replied Drinkwater.

George Curbishley who lived at Aston-by-Budworth wrote an essay on what he would buy his mother if given the money to spend. He wrote that he would buy her a pair of 'poots' which Mr Smith altered to boots. However, reading on a little further George mentioned feeding them with corn and the teacher was at a loss to know what to make of it. It transpired that his essay referred to a couple of 'pullets'.

Chapter Twelve ~~ The Rose Fete

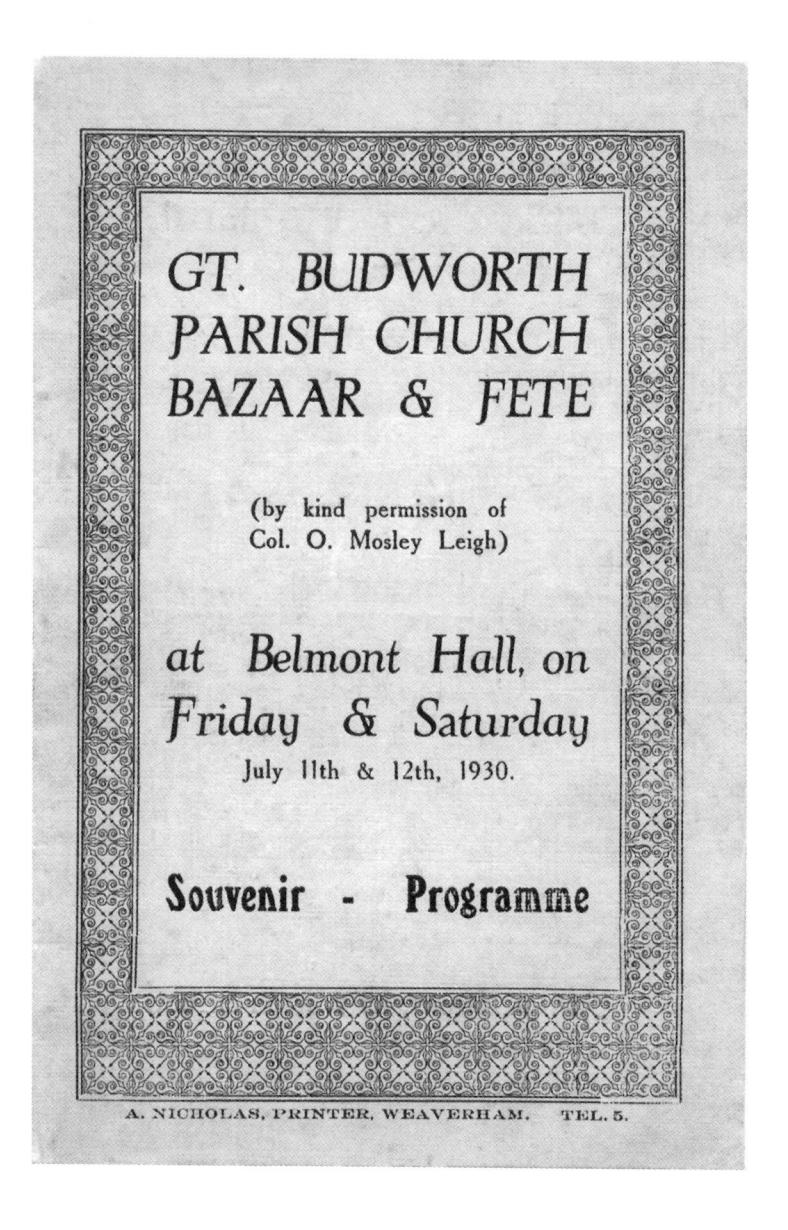

> **GT. BUDWORTH PARISH CHURCH BAZAAR & FETE**
>
> (by kind permission of Col. O. Mosley Leigh)
>
> at *Belmont Hall*, on *Friday & Saturday*
> July 11th & 12th, 1930.
>
> **Souvenir - Programme**
>
> A. NICHOLAS, PRINTER, WEAVERHAM.   TEL. 5.

After the first world war Great Budworth held an annual Rose Fete, often on the first Saturday in August, but this was discontinued after 1938. The venue for the Rose Fete was Belmont Hall Park and it was quite an event. A procession would leave the village marshalled by my late father and the late Dr Gilbert L Love and headed by the Northwich Adelaide Band (now disbanded). The morris dancers then followed dancing down the High Street. Then came all the characters in fancy dress, the Rose Queen bringing up the rear.

In the park there were the usual side-shows, hoopla, rifle range, bowling for a pig etc. and well-known sprinters came from a wide area to compete for valuable prizes.

In the Brunners' time, a concert party gave a performance on the lawn behind the hall. One performer, Leslie Flans, who was at the time a well-known member of the Northwich Amateur Operatic and Dramatic Society, used to tell a few funny stories. Here are two which I can remember.

He once related a story about a Sunday School which received an annual visit from the bishop. The children were all lined up and, as the bishop always asked the same questions each year, they were well schooled. On one occasion, however, the first little boy was absent and the second little boy was therefore to answer the first boy's question.

"Who made you?" asked the bishop

On receiving no reply he said, *"Come, come surely you know God made you."*

"Oh no he didn't," said the little boy, *"Him as God made is at home with tummy ache."*

The other story concerns a man who was in bed and near to death. He received a visit from a friend with whom he had played in the local band. During conversation the dying man said,

"Well Sam, I have about fifty pounds in the bank which I have decided to leave to you along with my gold watch and chain, but I should like to ask you what you consider to be the best two notes we have struck together in the old brass band?"

In reply his friend said, *"I think they be B sharp and D."*

In these pages I have endeavoured to recapture a few memories. All the characters mentioned have long since departed this life. I feel a debt of gratitude to them for providing a wealth of interest and variety to village life in an era that is past.

Alfred Worrall

Alfred Worrall wrote his first account in 1984 which he called 'In Living Memory'. This is printed without any editing. He then followed this with a further account which he called 'Interlude'. He included items which did not apply to Great Budworth and these have been edited out of this collection of memories. Alfred was born at 14 High Street, which was then called 'Mere View', in 1904. He was clerk to Great Budworth Parish Council from 1927 to 1934. He worked in agriculture and lived most of his later life in Hartford.

The Editors

Alfred Worrall as a young man - circa 1924

IN LIVING MEMORY
Alfred Worrall	Hartford 1984

At the beginning of the 20th century, life in the village of Great Budworth was completely different from life there now. Structurally the village is very much the same, still crowned by the fine old Church, but the lives of the residents are not comparable. Except for two or three or perhaps four or five old people still there, there will be none who shared the lives, the joys and the sorrows of the community of seventy or eighty years ago. No doubt that change has taken place in many many other villages, but Great Budworth is unique in a number of ways: it also happens to be the village where I lived.

It formed part of the large Arley Estate. Arley Hall, some three miles to the north, was the residence of the Egerton Warburton family so that we were all, including the farmers around, tenants. Perhaps most of the menfolk worked on the estate as joiners, wheelwrights, thatchers, painters, bricklayers, woodsmen and so on: each tradesman having a labourer. There were others classified as estate workers. Other men worked on farms or in the salt mine or on the salt pans across the fields at Marston, while several had found work on the rapidly growing chemical plant of Messrs. Brunner Mond & Company at Winnington.

The estate workers each had their own road length to trim or layer the hedges, clear the grass verges so that everywhere was always neat and tidy. We had the beauty and the joys of the avenues of lime trees, sweet scented in the springtime, with the noisy jays, the shrill-voiced shrikes, peewits, snipe and curlews in the meadow, while at night the hooting of the owls broke the silence. In the meadow below, from where the water supply to the village was pumped, we walked through bluebells and marsh marigolds under the full-blossomed wild cherry trees. Later each year, the avenue rustled with autumn leaves and girls played 'house' and danced their own dances. Boys were of sterner stuff and played 'Red Indians' and climbed trees along Farthings Lane.

In the field between the long avenue and Westage, there was a small well from which water for a small farm and a cottage was drawn. This well was also a place for frogs and just across Westage was a small pond known as 'Sally Walker's Pit'. Now who Sally Walker was we could never discover but were told that:

> Sally Walker sells fish
> Three ha'pence a dish
> If you want some come and buy some
> Sally Walker sells fish.

    Waterhens nested on Sally's pit and nearby was a farm track leading up to a sandhole; The Sandhole it was called, where Barney Birtles grew the best carrots for miles around and of which he was proud. Now this same Barney had a bull, an old one, about which to us boys there was something very mysterious, for when men from the village grew old, tired or lazy, people described them as being like Barney's bull ….. buggered.

    Every house had one or more raintubs collecting rainwater from spouts, etc. Domestic water was pumped from the meadow below the avenues to a tank in the garden of Providence House in Church Street and then fell by gravity to the five public taps in the village. Most noteworthy at that time was the long and widely renowned pump – BUDWORTH PUMP – where from the well-built and perfectly sited pumphouse at the bottom of Dene Hill was a constant supply of crystal clear water and where one could read:

> Blessings of never ending love,
> Are on us poured from heaven above
> This running stream with ceaseless flow
> Springs from the bounteous earth below.

    Outside the pumphouse was a trough where horses drank, while across the road was a playground with seats under the trees and alongside of which were the well-built and well-placed Dene Cottages on which inscriptions beseeched us to:

> Take thy calling thankfullie
> Love thy neighbour neighbourllie
> Shun the road to beggarie

Opposite these cottages and on the edge of the Dene woods was a babbling brook besides which campions danced in the breeze and a hawthorn displayed its red blossom. All this was a paradise of pure delight, full of legend, full of romance, where time stood still, where friends met friends and nowhere else in the whole world mattered. There are many who have travelled from far distant countries to revisit this place of childhood memories and I have a letter from one who emigrated more that seventy years ago and who has made plans that when her time comes her ashes will be flown home and scattered in the air over a Budworth field

Time will never dim the past
Too many memories hold it fast.

My great grandparents lived in Cob Cottage in Church Street, they were 'well on in the nineties'. The old man was of a very independent character, never known for politeness to no matter who. One Sunday he made the terrible mistake of putting a two shilling piece in the Church collection instead of the usual penny so therefore, marched to the Vicarage to tell Canon Holme what had happened and asked for one shilling and eleven pence change.

"*But my dear man,*" said the Canon, "*such a thing is not possible, it is not permissible or proper, to take back from the Lord that which has been given to Him, the Soul of a man so doing would be damned for ever.*"

"*Well Sir*", said the old man, "*Tha knows more abite that sort o thing than I dus, about his Soul bein damned an so on, but if I dunno get me one and eleven pence back I'll be buggered.*"

One day my father took me across to see them, the old man was down a passageway killing a duck. He cut its head off and the thing ran after me; I have never been so scared in all my life. Another day and as usual after dinner on Sunday, I went across with my father. He liked to 'keep an eye' on them. The old man was in his chair by the fire smoking his 'Churchwarden' pipe. The old lady was still at the table, leaning back in her chair. "*How is Gran?*" asked my Dad. "*A dusno know*" said the old man, "*A were just goin ter gie er a drink o water.*" She was buried the following Wednesday. The muffled bell had tolled twice.

For 'Upstreeters', those who lived in the higher part of the village, Church Street and School Lane, our playground was down 'The Butts', an unpaved way giving access to fields through which there was a pathway to Budworth Heath. The first was known as Brickie Field where in earlier years Yeomanry had rifle butts and where for a short time, bricks had been made, hence 'Brickie' pit where askers, jacksharps and tadpoles abounded. On the right hand side was a brook where watercress grew and where I believed the top part of the field was where Jesus Christ fed the five thousand, just as I believed that baby Moses had been hidden in the bullrushes in the reedbed by the Mere. A little way down 'The Butts' was a Smithy, always busy with the shoeing of horses, mending of ploughs, harrows, etc, etc. Sometimes when son Jim was out on an errand, boys would be allowed to blow the bellows, there was the clang of the hammer on the anvil, sparks flying from the red hot irons, the roar of the fire, the smoke and the smell of horses' hooves. What a wonderful world that was, a real world, thousands of times better than Disney and his like ever knew.

'The Butts' also formed a back road to Dene House, the Dower House of the Estate and the residence of the Usshers, a family said to have some relationship with the Egerton Warburtons. I never saw Colonel Ussher, it was whispered that he had not come home from the Boer War, but Mrs Ussher reigned in a grand manner no longer known. She gave Sunday School parties in a field along the drive which fronts Cock Lane. We had jellies and a sweet called 'blamange', as much as we could eat, cakes and lemonade ad lib. This benevolent old lady had a dog whose name was Togo, and Togo was a special dog because on Sunday mornings he shared a special cushioned pew in Church with Mrs Ussher. In winter times, Togo wore a lovely white woollen jacket and no matter how the ordinary dogs of the village wished to speak to Togo, he was not allowed to fraternise. Mrs Ussher had a kindly lady companion who called on village people in times of age, sickness or bereavement and read stories from the Holy Bible. One day, seeing the Bible on the table my father remarked,

"*I see Miss Pilkington has been. What has she been reading about this time?*"

"*Ooooooh,*" said the old man, "*Abite Jesus Christ an God an aw the so an so family on em.*"

I remember the banks of flowers in the Dene woods, the pride of Mr Hart the Head Gardener, snowdrops, crocus, daffodils, primroses, violets, just as I remember the first hybrid tea roses of Mr George Bowden.

In the village there were several 'Lofts' of homing pigeons and one job we had was to fly them around and then get them to loft quickly. On race days we had to dash off to Charlie Blackstock's Post Office and get them clocked in. I remember two winning birds we had, one we named 'Dole Cock' (remarkably enough this French city is now twinned to Northwich) and another we named 'Nellie's Queen', a lovely white-winged hen which won from Santander. What happened to the copper kettles which were the prizes, has long been a family mystery. Another hobby we had was fishing, Belmont Pool, Belmont Moat, the Dace pits at Budworth Heath, Ash pit, Coffin pit, Far pit, Gerrards pit and, by special permission, Arley Pool. Sometimes, with one of the Hall gardeners, we went secretly at night and used an acetylene light to throw a beam on to the float. One night we got a bucketful of fish, really good ones. Alas, alas this once lovely pool is no more, it was drained, so I was told, to lower the water level on the fields we knew as Priestners Knowls, so enabling them to be put to more profitable use. I wonder if on dark wet nights around the end of October, the eels – we called them snigs – migrate from one pit to another or to the brook like they used to do and as they did from the pool to the moat at Belmont.

I just remember a Wakes fair in Cook's field along Morkle lane, the flashing lights, coconuts, swings and hurdygurdy and the Coronation on the field opposite where there are now the pleasantly placed houses fronted by lime trees. I also remember the preparation and make-up of the soul-cakers and mummers, the fun and make-believe of it all. Will it ever be the same again I wonder? There was great excitement when Boss Porter was killing pigs: his yard was full of people and there was much ado, two most important men in white smocks, one of them with a large knife which he kept sharpened; the struggling and squealing of the pigs, the steaming tumbrel of scalding water, the blood for the black puddings, the boys on the outer ring waiting for the bladders and the dogs waiting for the melts or whatever else would be thrown to them. There were always sides of bacon on the ceiling of Porter's back kitchen which was also used as a dairy and this was where we were given beastings when cows calved and fermetty at the time of the Wakes.

Aerial photograph of the centre of Great Budworth
circa 1970

In the summertime, the playground of the villagers was down by the Mere, access to which was quite free and without restriction; we from Budworth had our section by the reedbed, Marston lads had their patch on Farish's field over the wire and Comberbachers through the cover (Covert) in the park. I don't think any of us had every heard of such things as trunks or bathing costumes.

Living in a village community one inevitably hears tales of the exploits of some of those who have gone before, the rather off-beat characters said by some to have 'bats in the belfry', 'a few loose tiles', to be 'round the bend', 'crackers' and so on. My late friend, Mr Cecil Holden in his book 'Our Village, Great Budworth 1700-1961', tells a number of these tales which made it evident that there was always someone or something to laugh at. A tale Mr Holden did not tell concerned Abie Littler, village layabout of the 1860s. Now Abie was not very articulate and he stammered, he was always at a loose end and no-one ever knew if he planned the story I relate. An elegant very smartly-dressed young gentleman came to the village. He was Curate to the Minister and lived at the Vicarage. One of his duties was to conduct the services at Pickmere Chapel and he, not knowing the way there, was taken by our friend Abie. Now why Abie lead the way through the meadow down to the brook running from Pickmere into Budworth Mere then through the boggy marshland we do not know but the going got very rough, the Curate's clothes wet and bespattered and he kept calling Abie a fool, an idiot and so on: Abie said he actually swore. The end of the story as told to me was that the Curate fell into the brook and got saturated, while Abie stood on the bank laughing at him, pointing down and saying "oo foo nar, eh?, oo foo nar?"

The George & Dragon I knew was a pub with sawdust on the floor; the landlord also stabled horses and ran a farm. It stands in a very good and prominent position, has a fine wrought iron sign with a sturdy bracket all made in the Arley Smithy. It depicts Saint George slaying the dragon and over the entry porch you may read:

> As Saint George in armed array
> Doth the fiery dragon slay
> So mayest thou with might no less
> Slay that dragon drunkenness

Drunkenness there was in those days; it was a frequent sight to see a man, not always an Irishman, asleep on the roadside or in a hedgerow several hours after closing time. What they drank was of course real beer, not the thin tasteless stuff of today and on which millions and millions of pounds are spent each year, trying to persuade people to drink it. It was a regular sight to see the wives of the salt workers waiting outside the pub early each Friday afternoon to catch their husbands before they went inside with their wages. Had they not done this the husbands would have arrived home drunk and penniless. At one time there were a number of pubs in the village but nowadays there is only the George & Dragon and this has become an hotel. Next nearest is The Cock, standing on a major road and perhaps thereby attracting more itinerants. At one time this was a rather famous coaching house where the itinerant 'Drunken Barnaby' and his like frequented. Among the rather spicy doggerel of Barnaby is a verse:

> Thence to the Cock at Budworth where I
> Drank strong ale as brown as berry
> Till at last with deep healths felled
> To my bed I was compelled.

'Johnny' Drinkwater was landlord of The Cock in the time of which I write, he also ran the farm. He was a colourful entertaining character and the stories he told would be as near the truth as is required from a successful horse-dealer, which was another of his trades. His patter transformed a jaded old hackney into the finest Arab steed and if he was with us today, any old jaloppy would become a Rolls Royce (someone had made a mistake and put the wrong name on it), which would purr along the motorways at two hundred and fifty miles an hour. It would only need just a spot of petrol every now and again and there are plenty of places which would be glad to let you have it.

One day at 'baggin' time, he was telling us that he made his money in horse-dealing. Old Phoebe misheard him and asked, *"Did you say horse stealing, mister?"* There was an explosion of such words that I cannot spell and I do not know if Phoebe ever got that week's wages.

The Church was the centre of the life of the village. St Mary and All Saints, formerly dedicated to God and All Saints, forms one of the finest examples of ecclesiastical architecture in Cheshire. Without doubt, the site has been used for worship from very early times – there was a priest present at the time of the Domesday Survey. It stands on a hill, it is imposing, handsome and impressive. It formed a large parish and at one time comprised seventeen townships with Chapelries at Witton and Lower Peover and was given by William, Constable of Chester and Baron of Halton, to the Priory of Norton in the reign of Henry I – about the year 1130. At the dissolution of the monasteries, the Rectory of Great Budworth, together with the Chapelries of Witton and Lower Peover, were presented to Christ Church, Oxford.

Interior of St Mary & All Saints Church

There had been restoration work but, apart from that, the Lady Chapel in the North transept is wholly 14th century and the historian Sir Peter Leicester records that, 'In this Lady Mary's Chappell aforesaid, was anciently the image of the Virgin cut in wood curiously trimmed and decked, her shoes gilded, hair fashioned on her head, set on a wood frame about two feet high. These idolatrous images were ordered to be removed out of all Churches upon the reformation of religion in 1538. The one at Budworth was taken down, hewed to pieces and burned in the Vicar's oven about 1559 by the command from Queen Elizabeth, who exerted herself to purge all Churches from what remained of those images.'

The Church is built of a pleasant red sandstone and the nave roof, dating from the early part of the 16th century is both effective and impressive. Great main timbers divide the roof into six bays and the rafters are well moulded. In the early part of the 18th century, there were at least two Chapels in the Church: St Mary's in the north transept and Arley Chapel in the south transept and which is exclusively appropriated to the Warburton family of Arley. There is a pleasing and well-proportioned west doorway, enriched with fine panelling surmounted with shields and flowers. In the high wall to the east of the nave can be seen where once was a doorway leading to a loft and I recall when as a child my grandmother telling me that she, or would it be her mother, remembered the loft above the chancel from which the choir sang?

From the Churchwardens' records, we learn that:

1751 Ralph Blease going to Limm to acquaint Mr Gatcliffe about the dial taking dimensions of the foundation.   1s 0d
1751 To Mr Gatcliffe, Mason for fixing up a dial in the Churchyard according to agreement.   £5 5s 0d
1753 To expenses in setting up stoops and rails about the dial. 1s 0d
(This sundial is by the south west porch, set on a circular stone.)

There are interesting items of Church furniture – two fine old chests, many and varied monuments which tell of the lives of notable people in days gone by.

Records show that the ring of bells were cast at Gloucester by A Rudhall 1733. One of the bells was recast in 1822. There are several inscriptions which read:

> 'I to the Church the living call and to the grave do summon all.'

> 'For George IV I raised my voice.
> His reign I'll ring, Budworth rejoice.'

> 'Prosperity to the Parish. AR 1733'

We were not so fearful in my time. To the rhythm and tone of the eight bells we joyfully sang:

> 'Why don't I go to Sunday School?
> Because I have no Sunday clothes.'

It still happens in places far away and wide that when the name of Great Budworth is heard, you will hear someone say, *"Oh yes, my grandparents, or my great-grandparents, were married there."*

What a history does the village hold, but now to my living memory. The festivals of the Church's year formed the calendar of what was a much more agricultural community than now. The timing of the work in the fields, ploughing, sowing, reaping and mowing, each had its own Patron Saint and we had a grand Harvest Home festival when the Church would be filled and decorated with farm and garden produce of all descriptions. What was eaten was largely according to season – we knew who grew early spring cabbage, who would have rhubarb and early potatoes, etc. We also knew of two poachers with large pockets, one of them, understood to come from Warrington or somewhere in that direction, was said to have a silent gun. Such matters were of course very secret, even from the good Lord Himself. In high social circles each kind of meat was according to season as was the freshwater fish. As time marched on, everything seemed according to plan and we were in step. In Church we sang:

> The rich man in his Castle,
> The poor man at his gate.
> God made them high or lowly
> And ordered their estate.

There are a number of books written by local historians, telling of the manners and customs of these and earlier times and I find them very interesting.

The lives of children were fully ordained: 10 am Sundays we met for prayers in school, by 10.30 we had crept silently into Church and sat in stalls behind the choir, creeping out silently just as the sermon was to begin. One day I dared to peep down the Church and ran home to tell my parents that I had seen Jesus Christ. It would be Canon Holme with his silvery grey hair standing in the pulpit. While the Egerton Warburtons – the gentry as they were called – had their own private chapel at Arley, they did, on special occasions, come to the Parish Church in their carriage and pair, complete with properly attired butler and ostler, the one to hand them from the carriage and the other to stable the horses at the George & Dragon. On these occasions we had been told to keep out of the way, keep out of sight, not to stand and stare. If the little girls were seen, they must curtsey and boys were to raise their caps. Before each Sunday Service peals of eight bells were rung, the second peal would stop five minutes before time so that the ringers, nearly all of whom were in the choir had time to hurry down from the belfry, walk along the north aisle to the vestry and so be ready for the service to begin. On winter evenings, a curfew was rung, the day had ended. Whenever a parishioner died a muffled bell was tolled, three times for a man, twice for a woman. When it happened to be one of the gentry, a muffled peal would be tolled at the funeral attended by the choir in newly washed snow-white surplices.

I recall a most memorable occasion. It was the evening of November 11th 1918 the first day the first world war ended. Without any prior notice at all, everyone came to the Church which was crowded, people standing in the aisles. The steeple rocked as the bells rang rapturously and we all sang 'NOW THANK WE ALL OUR GOD.' The bell-ringers and the men of the choir had their own joint supper. It was whispered that some of them had a glass of beer but this was never proved. We lads had a potato pie 'do' in the vicarage. This would be around Christmas time and in the summer we had a choir trip to New Brighton or Southport All children had 'stamp books' in which we placed stamps recording attendance at church on Sundays and on Saints' Days, of which there were many. To have a full book at the end of the Church's year was to qualify for entry in that 'Higher Kingdom' to which we all aspired. An awful lot was expected of us in those days, especially around Holy Week when we had a service every evening, two choir practices, one with the men and one by ourselves.

One lad, I will not tell you his name, said we should go on strike, which we did.

We stood along the rail beside the cottage at the end of School Lane and after a while the vicar marched out of Church, his cassock fluffing around his legs and went to our various homes. After a while fathers appeared on the scene and we heard *'Where's our Albert,' 'Where's our Ted,' 'Where's that lad of mine,' 'Where's our Alfie'* and we were all directed homewards to be dealt with according to the customs of the times. I remember hearing my mother saying *"That's enough dad, that's enough."* Whether or not the one who proposed the strike attained the Higher Kingdom or descended to the fires below I do not yet know. There was one boy afraid to strike and he crept into Church. Whether it was from fear of punishment in this world or the next I never knew. Time stood still for us lads in the choir, the words we sang were for the congregation, not for us. In any case the hymn 'Brief life is here our portion' has a bright jolly tune, while 'Rock of ages, cleft for me', 'A few more years shall roll' were words for the old folks down the Church. Nor were we concerned with the agony of the Jews in exile, they who 'Hung up their harps on the trees and sat down and wept by the waters of Babylon.' So lovely was the tune to that Psalm on the 28th evening that Babylon became a paradise.

None the less, yes, none the less there was a place we all feared; for some it was a place of terror, instant death was the punishment for trespass. It was a gravestone slab lying horizontal in the churchyard towards South Bank on which was inscribed:

> Stop your foot and cast an eye,
> As you are now, so once was I,
> As I am now so you will be,
> Prepare yourself to follow me.

We all trod very, very warily in that vicinity and, if in a dream we were drifting that way, we turned over and clung tightly to the bed rail.

The social life of the village comprised a Whist Drive and Dance, plus a 'Social Evening' at the time of the Wakes. Then, on Boxing Day, there was another Whist Drive and Dance, all these taking place in the school. On another and very special occasion there would be 'The Plays' which were entertainments given by the gentry and their friends in Arley Hall. These plays took the form of recitations, dialogues, one-act plays and perhaps a duet. Elevated indeed was the maid or maids invited to take part. In the village there was much enquiring, much wondering, much gossip, 'Have you heard?', etc, etc, for to receive an invitation to 'The Plays' was the hallmark of social status. Then each year just before Christmas, a bullock would be slaughtered and all those deemed needful and worthy would be invited to attend a room in the dairy to receive a gift of 'Bully Beef' attractively wrapped and handed to us by gentlefolk. This was a very happy occasion, for the room was decorated with holly and mistletoe. I remember also sweets and a drink of lemonade.

    I doubt very much if the people now living in Great Budworth realise the significance of this event to those of my early years for it is true to say that not all families had meat. Some did on Sundays with perhaps a little left over for lobscouse on Mondays, but some had no meat at all. However, there was kindness around – friends were seen taking 'something tasty' to where they knew it to be needed – a frock or coat which might fit your so and so, a doctor who forgot to send a bill.

    I have already told you of the Arley Plays, the Bully Beef and the fishing in the pool there, but as I knew the village pretty well then and some of the people who lived there, perhaps I may add a little bit more. My grandfather was a joiner and worked in the Arley estate for more than fifty years. On many Saturday mornings I walked with him by Hill Top Farm, down the old lane, across the fields and park to what was then the joiner's shop and to the saw mills where I saw huge tree trunks sawn and stacked in the timber yard. One Saturday morning job was to chop sticks, three full hampers, these for the fires in the hall over the following week. They had oil lamps in those days, electricity had not yet arrived. I well remember reading on a high wall:

> If proud thou be of ancestors,
> For worth or wealth proclaimed,
> So live that they, if now alive
> Of thee would not be shamed.

    Such noble thoughts were not for me of course. They were for a different sort of people but I had a grandfather who was a joiner and I chopped sticks on the shop floor. I also drank tea from his can lid and was it not the finest drink in all the world. Since those days of long ago, I have drunk wines in many countries, world-famous wines, but not one of them to be compared with the nectar I drank from the lid of my grandfather's tea can, which was blue. By having this drink I became a member of the company of the joiner's shop – Mr Miller worked there. Mr Curbishley called – a new handrail for the bridge

over the brook was required, a new post for the South Lodge where Mr Gatley lived; Mr Smith wanted a hinge for a door to the garden, the keeper – I forget his name – wanted a 'claphatch' for a gate along the old lane and Mr Ravenscroft said more fencing stakes were wanted along the hill by the Gore. So, as you see, the important affairs of the world were conducted from that joiner's shop, the mecca of my life. Once there was a very special occasion – two gentlemen (were they Mr Lewis and Mr Gorman?) called. A new stairway was required at a house called Sandilands, which was up through the lane of lovely red oaks a Crowley. It was urgent so I hoped and prayed every night that week, both to God Almighty and to Gentle Jesus, that I could go to Sandilands the next Saturday. My prayers were answered. What need had I for
ancestors? Let them stay hung up on the wall.

Living with my grandparents, I can say that 'we' had a pony and trap. As grandad grew older, we, that is grannie and myself, would go to Arley to meet him; later on grannie did not need to come. We went by the homes of friends – Dick Bebbington's at the end of the Westage, Dorothy Hughes at Royal Oak, Madge and Wilfred Gerrard's at Arley Moss Farm, Cath Gatley's at South Lodge, then through to the end of the park some two hundred yards from the joiner's shop. Here, if the gentry came along, I was to get out of the way and raise my cap. I could see the joiner's shop through those trees.

Back to Budworth now. Ours was a close and happy community, safe in our own world. Had we not rejoiced at the relief of Mafeking and, so it was said, won the Boer War? Pearson's Magazine had shown a picture of the enemy fleeing from Spion Cop and we still sang:

    Lord Roberts and Kitchener,
    General Buller and White,
    All gone to South Africa
    To have a jolly good fight.

    And when it is over
    Oh how happy we'll be
    The flag will fly over Pretoria
    And Kruger will hang on a tree.

Rule Britannia was our battle cry – we had an Empire on which the sun would never set.

However and alas, time marches on. Winds of change were in the air, we heard of emigration, people going overseas to far away parts of the Empire needing to be developed. We did in fact lose several families including the Wrights who had kept the George & Dragon Hotel and the farm therewith. Home Rule had become big news. Had we not a village doctor, a jovial, lively, flamboyant character named Gilbert Love who loved Ulster as much as he hated Popery and that was saying an awful lot.

Come into the ranks and fight for your King and Country – Don't stay in the crowd and stare

YOU ARE WANTED AT·THE·FRONT
ENLIST TO·DAY

Like all good Loyalists, he was ready to die for the Cause. Edward Carson was the Loyalist leader and he was recruiting an army to fight the Papists. The good village doctor used the well-known tactic of going into the public house, treating all around and then seeing all the men leave the pub wearing Carson's Army arm bands, all equally determined to shoot the so and so Pope.

However and alas again, time still marched and history now tells us that these men were not called for service in that particular army because those of military age were wanted elsewhere. The First World War had come and the running of German guns into Donaghadee by surreptitious means no longer mattered. Men from everywhere, including all Ireland, were needed to fight those terrible Huns as we then called the Germans. Posters were all around telling us 'Your King and Country Need You', of Kitchener pointing an accusing finger at YOU; recruiting sergeants prowled around, inviting chaps into the pub, buying them a drink and signing them on 'all for a bob a day'. White feathers were sent to those who did not answer the call, while men over forty years of age were given an arm band of another colour to save them from such indignity. Such affairs as these floated into the life of Great Budworth in the Year of our Lord 1914.

Politically we were, of course, solidly right. Who would think or dare to be otherwise? Yet from beyond our boundaries came whispers and rumours of other doctrines, doctrines subversive to our long-established way of life. It was said that both Mr Brunner and Mr Mond were foreigners and, worse than that, they were Liberals with their hated doctrine of Free Trade. We were taught to sing:

> Ours is a happy land,
> Some people say,
> There is a happy land,
> Far, Far away,
> And while we get the dump
> Causing our commercial slump,
> Trade flies away.

The name of Lloyd George swept into our Tory stronghold. It was said that one of our landlord's family enquired of the village postmaster, *"Who is this – er – er – who is this George Lloyd?"* We had been told that he was a noisy little braggart from Wales and taught to shout:

> Lloyd George, no doubt
> When his life ebbs out,
> Will ride in a golden chariot,
> And sit in state on a red hot plate
> Twixt the Devil and Judas Iscariot.
> Ananias that day,
> To the Devil will say,
> Sit up a bit higher away from the fire
> And make room for that Devil from Wales.

    We were in the Year of our Lord, 1914, the year that saw the start of the first World War. That 'noisy little braggart from Wales' was soon to become Prime Minister, but let us move on four years or so, for no doubt you have read books and heard first hand stories of that most terrible tragedy. My story is about Great Budworth and its people. There was anguish, broken homes, broken hearts, hearts which never could be mended just as there were in villages and towns all over the country, in fact all over the world.

    Two lads from Budworth, one named Frank, a little on the shortish side, told me how he and thousands of others were being discharged at a port in Northern France; a Major General was addressing them through a microphone, telling them of the glorious victory they had won, how they had been fighting for the greatest, grandest, the most noble Empire the world had ever known. Frank said that by the time the speech ended he felt he was standing on a tub about ten feet high................. The other lad, his name is on the plaque in the Lych Gate, did not come home. He had been awarded the Military Cross for an act of bravery. A high-ranking Officer brought the medal to his home. His mother told the Officer he could keep it. It was her boy she wanted.

    I began this little 'In Living Memory' story with the remark that life in the village of Great Budworth is now completely different from that of the early years of this century and I have recorded some of my experiences and recollections of that time. You may ponder as to which kind of life you would prefer, the close community of neighbours or the much wider and largely pagan world of today.

Alfred Worrall
Hartford 1984

Alfred Worrall
INTERLUDE
Hartford 1984

Alfred Worrall aged about 40

When I first wrote these 'In Living Memory' stories a short while ago they were intended for a few friends, I had no idea of there being a wider interest or demand, or of recording more stories over a longer period. It came about, however, that a resident of the village suggested I had more copies printed, these to be sold and the total proceeds donated to the Church Restoration Fund and this I was pleased to do. Now I have requests for still more copies and for further recollections of Great Budworth and its people. Just as I intended it, the first little book told of village life up to the time of the 1914-1918 war which did indeed see the end of an epoch. Perhaps you will agree with me that there could be no better way of linking the two periods of my book, and noting time and events marching on, than by extracts from Parish Magazines. These are taken from the period 1914 to March 1921 when the Church still had considerable influence, both religious and social, over the affairs of the village and its people. So here is my selection:-

September 1914	Since our last issue our Country with almost the whole of Europe has been plunged into the most terrible and far reaching war in history. The British Nation was obliged in honour to take up arms. A month ago peace, today WAR. I put the word in capital letters for such a war never before has been seen and, please God, never will become possible. Do we in any serious sense realise what this war means to us, what are we fighting for? To help France say some, to fulfil a treaty obligation to Belgium say others. Both these answers are true, but only partially true. The big answer is that we are fighting for our very own National existence.
October 1914	Formation of the Prince of Wales Fund War Relief Committee. Monthly house-to-house collections.
Nov 1915	A Detachment of the Volunteer Training Corp is formed. The vicar is Commander, Mr H S Smith, Secretary, Platoon Sergeant - J Scott.
June 1916	Women's work in war time; Many opportunities for women and girls to learn farming and gardening and so free men for service with the colours.
Oct 1916	A new Squad of Great Budworth Volunteers. Review by Lord French at Chester. Bravery awards to Henry Hubbard and Arthur Mather, but Henry Hubbard was killed.
June 1917	DCM for Charles Lever.
April 1918	Albert Hughes loses a leg by accident down Dene Hill. £6. 2s. 0d. proceeds of Dance Fund to help.
May 1918	Names of lads killed on active service. Several more bravery awards. Collections for the Albert Hughes fund now reached £40.0.0. which paid for an artificial leg.
August 1918	'Bob' Adair died of wounds in Salonika. 'Jimmy' Shingles awarded MM.
September 1918	Sympathy to Mrs Johnson and Mrs Harrop whose husbands have been killed.

December 1918	Armistice day brought news that Fred Naylor had laid down his life for his Country. 'A fine lad, a good son, one of the first to volunteer for service. His death is a sad loss for his mother and family and all our sympathies go out to them. It may be some comfort to know that he was one of those whom God allowed to come home to say 'goodbye'.'
December 1918	James Henry Hulme and Alan Atkinson. These two gave their lives, all they had, for liberty. God rest their souls.
.June 1919	Final meeting of the Soldiers' and Sailors' Fund. Mr H S Smith, who has returned to his post as Schools Headmaster, expressed thanks for all that had been done while they were away on active service.
August 1919	PEACE CELEBRATIONS IN GREAT BUDWORTH. What was generally described by those who witnessed it, and there were many visitors from a distance, as far and away the most striking demonstration associated with Mid-Cheshire Peace Festivities, took place in the beautifully quaint village of Great Budworth on Saturday.
In point of size Great Budworth ranks among the smallest of Cheshire villages, its population being scattered, yet associated with Aston and Pickmere it put the blush to many big towns, celebrating the greatest event in history.
A masterly achievement. Belmont Park, by kind permission of Mr & Mrs Roscoe Brunner was used. The Chairmanship of Dr Gilbert Love who made a masterly speech of thanks and welcome home. Treasurers were the Rev F L Smithett and Mr P M Armitage. Catering Mrs J McIntyre. Events programme Mr S Worrall. Speech also by Major Renwick. The Northwich Adelaide Band played. Many thanks to Mr & Mrs Roscoe Brunner who suitably responded.

(Not in the Church magazine but quoting what was said at the time: 'When the head of the procession was in the park it stretched to the bottom of Dene Hill.')

April 1920	Gave the names of men who have fallen and of men and women (four) who also served.
March 1921	Opening and Dedication of the Lych Gate by the Lord Bishop of Chester, with tablets containing the names of those who had fallen and of those who served, unveiled by Lt Col Geoffrey Egerton-Warburton, DSO.

Perhaps I should here refer to comments made on several items from the first part of my book, comments which I am very pleased to have. Firstly then, several people tell me that the sign of St George & the Dragon outside the hotel of that name was made in Nurenburg and the sturdy bracket alone made in the Arley smithy. I had understood it was all made at Arley. Referring to what I wrote about The Butts and Brickie Field, my friend Mr Harry Foster tells me that Brickie Field was also known as Brickle Field – possibly a corruption of Brick Hill. I had said that The Butts was so called because of use by the Yeomanry but Mr Foster tells me that since there are indentations in some of the stones around the south door of the Church, which could have been made by mediaeval archers sharpening their arrows, it is possible that The Butts, as archery butts, predated the use of the field by the Yeomanry by several centuries.

I have learned of another possibility of the origin of the indentations which is that they may be votives, representing a pledge or a prayer for the safe return from a shrine or a pilgrimage overseas. How interesting it would be if we had sagas of mediaeval families in the Icelandic style.

And then I hasten to correct any wrong impression I gave of Arley Pool for, after being almost dried up for a number of years, it has been restored although not so large as it was.

With the ears of a child one heard the single bell for each daily morning and evening service and the Church clock strike each quarter hour. We would see someone hurrying to Church; we were in our own world. In our world we had regular visitors, butchers, bakers and candlestick makers, and when we saw them we knew which day it was, these good tradesmen knowing and being known by the families concerned. In cases of hardship good measure was given. Paraffin oil, of course, wicks and pans. Mr Pickering with crumpets, Mr Sandbach with shoe laces, cottons, buttons, needles, odds and ends. His technique was to knock on the door and be greeted by 'not today thank you Mr Sandbach' but his box was already open on the step so the door could not be closed and by the time he had asked the welfare of the little baby, and the items in the box had been turned over, the housewife would be pretty sure to see something she needed. A 3d or 6d sale was good business. Then we had Mr Cowap – using a modern term he was 'upmarket' from the others because he sold dress materials, silks and satins for ladies. I remember his telling me how proud I should be to be British; he had heard of the battle of Jutland and how we had been sinking German battleships to the bottom of the sea.

There were other itinerants, gypsies with clothes pegs, little brushes, windmills, tops, etc, etc. They also cast spells and read palms, tracing long lines which, to young ladies not yet betrothed, foretold a voyage across the seas and somewhere in the shadows there was a tall dark handsome young gentleman with a dowry of an almost unbelievable thousand pounds a year. All this for only sixpence! There was a man with a tin whistle, another with an accordion, one with a barrel organ – we called it hurdy-gurdy – with a monkey on top.

The man who called 'kittles ter mend, sithers and knoives ter sharpen' and when he upturned his little contraption he spun the wheel and the sparks did fly.

He would *'loike a drink of hot water Mrs'* – but he loiked it better with tea in it!

Then the rags and bones man, any old iron, any old iron – *'O'll be pleased to take it out of your way Mrs.'*

79

We may get a balloon, maybe a block of salt or donkey stone or raddle for the step. Friendly folk were these itinerants, possibly plying their way from one parish workhouse to another, or perhaps they knew a barn or a cosy hedgecop somewhere. Roads were narrow, grass verges were wide and cows, here and there a goat, would graze on what is still known in Ireland at any rate as 'the long pull'. That was our world, a community of friends and neighbours. What is there now? Motor cars, aeroplanes, satellites, supermarkets and soon we are to have hypermarkets instead. I have recently been to the United States of America. I put coins in the slot and out came the goods, neatly parcelled, and the change. I spoke to nobody, no not I, and nobody spoke to me.

I was a few months older than Drinkie so left school before him. While at school, each of us would have a special pal or chum for a while at any rate and one such of mine was Drinkie, a mixture of a lad if ever there was one. Warm-hearted, pleasant, easy going, always following the line of least resistance. Even so, there always seemed to be something stirring when he was around. The school headmaster arranged a weekly race for the boys, through both Avenues, back along Westage and Farthings Lane to school. Drinkie won the first two weeks but on the third it was discovered that he knew a gap through the hedge on the long avenue which cut about one hundred yards off the distance. He never won again. Resuming school one afternoon, the Headmaster called out *"Drinkwater, come to the front I want a word with you"*. Drinkie, on the back row and out of the way as always, spluttered *"p.p.p.p.please Sir, I've not been smoking"*. The scene ended with him standing in front of the class with a cigarette in his mouth, a box of matches in one hand and a packet of Woodbines in the other.

At age 15, I was on shift work in the time office of HM Factory, Victoria Works, Wincham and, because there was a public house between where the man supposed to be in charge lived and the time office, I was often in charge myself. Drinkie became my assistant and for some reason unknown to me was not put on staff grade. Consequently he was paid about twice as much as me. A generous hearted lad he was; said that this was not fair and that we should divide his excess and spend it on pork pies and Coral Flake tobacco at Mrs Bowden's shop. This we did for two or three weeks I think, but then he achieved promotion to the position of 'can lad' for Jimmy White's navvy gang and we lost touch. Dear old Drinkie, never short of 'Spanish' (liquorice) or treacle dabs – ten a penny from Emma Boardman's at the Post Office. No-one ever knew which bank he used.

When reading the magazine extracts you would note the activities of the Soldiers' and Sailors' Presents Fund, of which my father (Samuel Worrall) was Secretary. It was to him that acknowledgements and letters of thanks would be sent and these letters were read to the Committee in the upper room of the Reading Room. How or why it came about I do not remember but sometimes I had the job of reading them. Most were expressed in the sincere and simple language of the time - saying many thanks, asking of news of other lads they knew to be in the forces, as to the welfare of this or that young lady of their fancy, or saying what they would do when they came home – go fishing on the Mere and such things as that. It came about, however, that there was one letter of quite a different calibre, the exact meaning of which had to be explained to one or two members of the Committee. This letter concluded, 'Reiterating the aforesaid expression of thanks, Yours sincerely, F C Astles'. (I remember one committee member asking, 'wot the 'ell does that mean, wot's he torkin abite?')

Some time after the war I met Fred in the village – he was in uniform and very smart. I learned that he was a 'Military Accountant' and could not think of ever coming back to live in the village. Military service was to be his career. Maybe someone reading this will know more of Fred's subsequent life than I do, for many years went by before I heard the name again. This was when the name of Major 'Bob' Astles – son of Fred – Military Adviser to General Idi Amin of Uganda – hit the headlines of the whole world telling of mass murders of prisoners, shootings, escape across the river in a fast boat on a dark night and so on. There was talk of trials and prosecutions but no more have I heard. What has become of General Idi Amin of Uganda and his Military Adviser, Major 'Bob' Astles, whose father was born and bred in Great Budworth, I do not know. Perhaps some future historian of Great Budworth would care to investigate. Perhaps also it would be wise to take care!

Maybe the same future historian, lady or gent, would like to find out what has become or what became of the instruments of the one time village brass band. The last I heard was that, during the incumbency of the Rev Leslie Evans (1950), there was a tidy up in the attics of the Old Vicarage and some were found and removed – where to I do not know. Can they be packed among all the souvenirs in the upper Reading Room I wonder? Personally, I do not recall ever hearing of a village band but a story told by the late Mr Foster senior was of an occasion when members of the band had been taking part in a competition in Manchester. They returned to Lostock Gralam station on the last train having 'looked upon the wine when it was red' and marched back to Budworth playing in full force.

Having reached the running pump at the bottom of Dene Hill, the conductor stopped them and said, 'Now lads, we must not wake up the village at this time of night, so let us take our boots off!' This they did, slinging them round their necks with the laces. Then they marched through the village playing God Save the Queen. That, I am told was about the year 1881.

Other than the absolute certainties of our Christian belief, there was an area of superstition and other-worldliness about which we could not be quite so sure. There were quite a few 'will-o-the-wisp' stories around and, perhaps because of the romance attached, that of the Marbury Lady, that once beautiful Egyptian princess, was the most prominent by far, and generally accepted. In addition to the romantic aspect there is real evidence to confirm the facts on which the stories are based.

James Hugh Smith-Barry (1748-1901) was a member of a family steeped in the traditions of aristocracy, widely known as gamblers, cock-fighters, huntsmen, etc. Besides Marbury they had other estates, including one in Ireland where Bacchanalian revelries became part of Irish social history. It is known that here in Marbury there have been ice festivals on the frozen mere, not on the scale of Virginia Woolf's phantasy of Orlando, on the Thames – that would be impossible – but nonetheless with four thousand or more on the ice, with roasting carcasses, real old-time barbecues with gallons of rum, beer, etc, ad lib – such were the generosities of the Smith-Barry family.

Now James Hugh treasure-hunted far and wide and many were the treasures he brought home – and this is where our Marbury Lady first comes to the scene. He had fallen in love with this beautiful darkie girl, a real princess; he proposed to her and promised everything he had (I would have loved to have heard his protestations) if she would come to England and marry him - his world would be hers.

Alas, alas, the chroniclers record that his ardour cooled, back home himself he had found another bedmate. The princess arrived and was broken-hearted; he promised her many things but broken hearts are not mended like that. She refused to return to Egypt and time marched on. The wife of James died and, perhaps with shame, I don't think it would be in triumph, they did cohabit. Over the years they had five children and it is on record that it was only by Royal Licence that these children were allowed to bear the arms and name of Smith-Barry. When the princess died her body was first buried at Great Budworth but soon there was much disturbance around Marbury. In the hall, bells would ring in the servants' quarters, there were tremors throughout the whole buildings, beds would shake, pictures would fall, movement and 'presence' was felt. Perhaps because of what had been agreed between them, James Hugh had the body exhumed and brought to Marbury where it was later mummified but those strange hauntings and visions did not cease. For two hundred years now there have been visitations. The courtyard clock can no longer rattle and shake at the midnight chime as it once did, because it is no longer there but, if you walk by the old mill some time, or in the park along the mereside, through the shadows of the big wood, or where the courtyard once was you may hear echoes or see and feel the presence of the spirit of this once lovely Marbury Lady. I suggest you read St John 3, Chap 3.

Villagers with church bells 1922

Are these stories 'will-o-the-wisp' though? For here is one which tells of a ghost which visits the Quaker burial ground at Whitley. Late one night three men were travelling home in a motor car – they had been to a business meeting, not to a public house – when approaching the burial ground they each saw the figure of an elderly lady dressed in white leaning on the wall; they saw her quite clearly in the headlights of the car. They stopped just beyond, not knowing what to do. One man suggested that they walk back to investigate or to help, but another said he was scared and wanted nothing to do with it, so reluctantly they drove on. Of those three men, only one is still alive and I have been to see him this very evening. He is still absolutely emphatic of the truth of what I have told you, as, he says, were the other two, right to their dying days. It is said that this ghostly lady visits that same place each twenty-five years. Why that should be the frequency I do not know but, if any of you are really interested, I suggest you visit the lounge of the Chetwode Arms Hotel, Whitley sometime and ask the locals for more information.

There is the ghost of Peck Mill, quite near to where I lived for a number of years. Living and working at the mill was the farmer/miller with his two sons who were very fond of a joke. One night, teasing their father, one of them dressed himself in a white sheet and walked in the wood, while the other climbed a tree and made calls. Hearing this, the father took out his gun and shot the 'white ghost'. His son was dead but his ghost appears at times. This happened in the days when horses still provided transport and many were they who shimmied, shied and neighed when over the brook on the road between the mill and the wood. Were they in the 'presence'?

I recall a story told to me by my grandfather of a Ghostly Spirit which appears once each year on the road between Royal Oak Cottage, Aston and Hill Top Farm. The road was then known as Grindeck Lane. This ghost appears on each anniversary of a 'moonlight flit'! Something was lost on that 'moonlight flit'. Was it a child or who else was it? No-one seems to know but the ghost still searches.

Now just another thought of the Marbury Lady. One dark, wet night Mr Jimmy Hughes (of Porter's Yard) and another workman were walking home across the park. Jimmy was of a very nervous disposition. At the foot of the wood below Brownslow was a large holly bush and, on reaching the gate, Jimmy distinctly heard a rustling and a flap-flap-flap. No doubt with the Lady in mind he turned and ran right back across the park and home via Comberbach. Jimmy's friend did not run but found the village 'Bobby' by the holly bush shaking the rain off his cape!

The years of the Great War had come and strange and wonderful were the tales we were told. There were those who had a friend who had a friend who knew someone who had seen many train loads of Russian troops with snow on their boots and helmets, having come over the North Pole down through Scotland, travelling through England on their way to the battlefields in France.

There was a searchlight at the top of Dark Lane and its beam swept the sky. I was told, and knowing the people concerned would say that it could be true, that Mr Hulme of Lands End Farm lost a calf and was swearing. Now Mrs Hulme, a pious person, seeing the beam of the searchlight swishing through their trees was frightened and told him that the vengeance of the Lord was coming upon him. One night I was one of a party walking home from work; we were at the top of Farish's long field when the searchlight swept through the trees. Jimmy Hughes (of Porter's Yard) ducked and swore saying, *'If them .... are not careful they'll be 'ittin somebody at top o't yed with them .... things.'* Inevitably during the time of war forebodings and rumours of calamities are rife and there was one of these most persistent. There was a High Explosives Factory at Gadbrook, Northwich, at which many locals were employed. Some of these used to swear that framed in the sky over the factory they had seen 'the angels of Mons' on more than one occasion. Because that is now so long ago there may be some of you who do not know that Mons was the scene of dreadful casualties to our troops. Hence the vision of 'angels'.

A little earlier I told you that other than the absolute certainties of our Christian belief there was an area of other-worldliness and superstition and I have related a few stories which belong to that area. You may or may not accept them. You may say they are not true but I tell you that some of them are well founded. They form part of the folklore, legend and traditions of the time, as difficult to prove as to disprove. There are, as Norman Collins said, 'facts of fiction'. Let us turn another page.

Memories of Great Budworth ~ ~ Alfred Worrall

For you to enter into our changing way of life it may be a good idea to give you the programme of our Wakes Social – held in the school in November 1920 – and to include comments I wrote in my diary at the time. These comments were not intended as criticism of any one in any way. They were written in a light-hearted way, just for the fun of it.

Great Budworth Wakes Social Programme – 14 November 1920

1	Sketch entitled	'PC Lievesley'	Mr G Hubbard
2	Song	' Sheep Shearing'	Mr F Thurlwell
3	Part Songs	'Alan Water' & 'Larboard Watch'	
			Messrs W Mellor, F Eyres, S Dunn & E Dickens
4	Songs	'Pale Hands I Loved' & 'My Friend'	Mr G B Shingler
5	Song	'Comin' thru' the Rye'	Miss F Hitchen
6	Mime & Dialogue		Rev F L Smithett
7	Song	'Tinker, Tailor, Soldier, Sailor'	Miss Amy Jones
8	Song & Patter	'A Spot of Nonsense'	Miss Dolly Worsley & Mr F Thurlwell
9	Song	'When You Played the Organ'	Mr H Gibbon
10	Songs	'The Old Shako' & 'When the Red Light Shines Bright'	
			Messrs J & E Lever
11	Songs	'Let the Rest of the World Go By' & 'My Ain Folk'	
			Mr 'Jock' McKensie

During the interval and while refreshments are being served, Mr Leonard Worsley will be at the piano and play Sonatas (Haydn) and Preludes (Chopin Op 24). In a lighter vein he will lead you in Community Singing with songs of the day including 'That Wonderful Mother of Mine', 'God Send you Back to Me', 'Romany Rose', 'There's a Long, Long Trail a Winding' and 'When Irish Eyes are Smiling'.

The Rev Paterson Morgan (as guest of Dr Gilbert Love) will move a vote of thanks to the artists and offer a few words of advice.

13	Sketch	'Oh Mr Porter'	Mr G Hubbard
14	Songs	'Ma, He's Kissing Me' & 'Chase me Charley'	
			Mr (Starchy Joe) Millington
15	Songs	'If Those Lips Could Only Speak'	Mr Albert Holden
16	Songs	'When the Gread Red Dawn is Shining' &	
		'Till the Sands of the Desert Grow Cold'	Mr Thurlwell
17	Song	'Many Brave Lads are Asleep in the Deep, so Beware, Beware'	
			Mr C Holden
18	Part Songs	'Annie Laurie' & 'Linden Lea'	
			Messrs W Mellor, F Eyres, S Dunn & E Dickens
19	Songs	'Mending Roadways' & 'Moira My Girl'	Mr G B Shingler

20	Song	*'Trumpeter, What are your Sounding Now'*	
		Mr C Holden, Mr Worsley, piano and Mr Mellor, trumpet	
21	Song	*'Take a Pair of Sparkling Eyes'*	Messrs J & E Lever
22	Songs	*'The Bells of St Mary's' & 'Who is Sylvia'*	Miss Amy Jones
23	Song	*'Smiling Through'*	Miss F Hitchen
24	Dialogue	*'Mind Your Own Business'*	Mrs E Garner & Miss Dolly Worsley
25	Recitation	*'The Wreck of the Hesperus'*	Mr G Hubbard
26	Songs	*'Why am I Always the Bridesmaid?' & 'Cos I'm Only a Working Man'*	
			Mr F Thurlwell

<u>THE KING</u>

There was an extra item during the programme – a Monologue entitled 'Loony versus Boony'. Loony (Spencer of Marston) and Boony (Red Lion, Pickmere) telling of a digging match which Boony won. 'Jock' McKensie was both author and narrator.

The biggest hit of the evening was Gilbert Hubbard's first number. As he was getting on to the stage the steps collapsed and he fell neck and crop right across it. The audience thought he was acting (he hurt his leg quite badly) and screamed with laughter. Mrs Barber fell off her chair, Grannie Thompson lost her teeth, Old man Barber said, *'Wots he torkin abite a canna err im'*. Jock McKensie went on the stage to help and Hubbard was heard to say, *'Holy Hell, my .... leg'*. Later, when the same Hubbard announced *'The Wreck of the Hesperus'*, he said he had forgotten who wrote it but, after a few lines, he was interrupted by Charlie Squires. Then he said to the audience, *"Charlie said it was written by Longfellow. I knew it was by some tall bloke but I couldn't remember his name."*

Doorkeepers were Messrs Dick Cocksey, Sam Worrall, Nucksie Dickens and Ralph Platt. 'Nucksie' was heard to say, *'Shut that door Sam, they ought ter ave a leet in that winder, av nearly brock my .... leg.'* Sam Worrall asked if them so and so's by that biler av getten any tickets. Cocksey said *'Nucksie and me's going ter fetch Southern. Ee said ee were goin ter feed is rappits byt its teckin im a'ell of a while.'* Gilbert Love came through the doors saying that McDonald & Snowdon were traitors and the so and so's ought to be shot. Then, seeing Padre Smithett said, *'Sorry Frank, I did not see you there'*.

Morgan's advice during the interval was to the effect that the secret of success was to practise elocution in the bathroom every morning, marry a rich man's daughter and live happily ever after. He was interrupted by 'Comrade' Holden who told him that not everyone had a bathroom and that there weren't enough rich men's daughters to go round but *'when tha's getten gift oft gab like the's got and married one tha'll land in hell afore tha's finished'*. Gilbert Love started singing 'Rule Britannia', Comrades Holden and Tom Hubbard countered with 'The Red Flag' but were soon drowned out. Holden shouted, 'All ye like sheep are lead astray' and Jimmy Hughes said, 'If yer dunno vote fo't Doctor he winna get yer better.'

While Frank Thurlwell (the Frank mentioned on the last page of the first part of the book) was on the stage receiving loud applause, grins all over his face, a certain young lady sitting next to his mother told her that, 'It's all right your Frank standing there, everybody clapping and him looking all innocent like that, but I could tell you a thing or two about him if I wanted to. *"Eh lassie,"* said his Mother, *"that dunno worry me, I should be a darn sight more worrit if he's bin where ee as bin and adna larn't a thing or two."*

Alfred Worrall sitting on the step outside Mere View, 14 High Street, 1909

A long-established custom had been the regular gathering of the men of the village along the rail by the cottage at the end of School Lane, always after they had been home and had their tea, as it was called in those days. The events and affairs of the day would be discussed always in the vernacular, other pronunciations or idioms would be foreign to them. Youngsters would not dream of daring to join them – their place was on the sandstone sills of the pump house opposite. Ralph Platt was the first man in Great Budworth to wear brown shoes – they were new and, like all new shoes in those days, they squeaked. Quite a stir they caused, and quite a subject of conversation. BBC English was not known on either side of the road for it was not yet born. Promotion occurred when a lad took to long trousers and he dared to be seen smoking, then he would cross the road and learn of the mysteries of life about which no doubt the men would be talking. Later in the evening the men would go across to the George & Dragon to pay their tontine, so they said. Wives were never seen, of course – their place was at home. Such was the order of things in those days of long ago.

But here we were in the 1920s – the gay 20s as they were later called – when the Charleston came. You have seen the programme of the concert with songs old and new, some gay, some sentimental, the tuneful harmonies of the Marston quartet and the patter of the humorists. What a mixture – but so seemed our world. Mr W S Gilbert told us, *"When everyone is somebody then no-one's anybody."* So what did it matter? Ladies no longer wore crinolines, girls had their hair 'bobbed', gentlemen forsook spats and lads wore 'Oxford bags'. Pony traps had gone and so had wagonettes. Lightfoots no longer ran them from the bottom of Dene Hill on market days – Northwich 6d return, lads 3d. Buses had come, so had gramophones, but Adam Boardman no longer ran the Royal Mail Northwich to Crewe – what became of those prancing 'high steppers'? Gentry no longer were seen in their landaus, complete with ostler and footman but farm tractors came, though not to Fred Renshaw's – he would not have them on his land because he said they created a hard pan of earth which prevented the proper growing of crops. Moving pictures had come to Northwich and Warrington. The films were very different from John Bunyan's story of Pilgrims' Progress which, by the grace and favour of Mr William Leigh (of Marston Common) and his Magic Lantern, we saw each winter.

Mary Pickford had become the 'world's sweetheart' and Rudolf Valentino the 'great lover'. We sang 'When Irish Eyes are Smiling'; Gracie Fields brought 'Sally' into all our homes. The war was over, the boys were home again' – some of them that is – and some of these with girl friends from elsewhere. We still had land girls around and girls on the domestic staff of Mrs Ussher of the Dower House and other large houses around. All this resulted in new names, new faces and new ideas. Long-established local customs and traditions dissolved. Such was our world of the 1920s.

Our parish was within the area of the Runcorn Rural District Council and it had come to pass that for a period I acted as clerk to the Parish Council. I believe my salary was thirty shillings per annum, which included payment for two journeys to Frodsham for inspection and audit of the books. The main purpose of the council was the maintenance of the established order of things, the distribution of several charities usually left to the discretion of the Vicar and Mr McIntyre.

Tramps passed through the village much less frequently than at one time and it was the business of the village constable to see them safely on their way to Dutton workhouse where they would spend maybe an hour or two breaking stones to recompense for their sojourn.

At our meetings there could be whispered undertones of an unwanted baby but this was hardly a matter for discussion between gentlemen. For the girl in distress there would be a friend somewhere, or so it was hoped. Such things were not entered in the minutes, our business was more to do with rates and precepts.

Some villagers were becoming astir; we should have electric lights in our houses and in the streets, the days of paraffin lamps were over and we needed water in our homes. *'Wot would it put ont rates?'* one stalwart councillor would always ask and another repeated that he had carried water from the Dene all his life and 'hard work never did anyone any harm'. There had been some correspondence with the Northwich Electricity Supply Company and we had been told of the minimum usage and number of points necessary before they could come. Mr Harry Walton – by far the most energetic and active member of the council and also a member of the Runcorn RDC – had been in touch with Dr Hunter (I think that was his name), the Medical Officer of Health to that council, in regard to a water supply but, once again, it was decided to defer the matter to our next meeting.

I did not follow these instructions, I did exactly the opposite and invited Mr Fennell and Dr Hunter to come to discuss matters. Meetings were arranged and Mr Fennell and Dr Hunter came. Quite soon thereafter we had both electricity and water and we no longer needed 'cats' whiskers' for our 'wireless' sets. Mr Walton knew but no other member of the council even asked how it came about.

When I had written the first part of this book I had no thought of writing more – this I told you in the Interlude. I also told you that if I did add to the stories then the time sequence could be lost and this seems to have happened. Looking over what has been written I find that I have not told you anything of the history and legend of that wonderful hound 'Bluecap', or of those great horses 'Marbury Dunn', 'Spinner' and 'Bergamot', all of Marbury. (Perhaps my thoughts were too much concerned with the history and tragedy of the once lovely Lady.)

Firstly then, Bluecap, owned by Mr John Smith-Barry (1725-1784) renowned leader of his pack of hounds. As we already know something of his character and activities, we know that the fame of Bluecap would be boasted far and wide. His speed was matchless as was his stamina, so much so that neither stags nor hares were good enough – only foxes could provide a worthwhile chase. It was from his time that hounds became known as foxhounds. In 1772 Mr Smith-Barry challenged Mr Hugo Meynell, Master of the Quorn Hunt, to provide two hounds to race with Bluecap and his offspring named Wanton. The race was run at Newmarket with five hundred guineas as the stake – a lot of money in those days. Bluecap was first, Wanton was second. There are a number of stories of wagers and races won but, alas, though history and legend remain, Bluecap died at the age of thirteen years. An obelisk was erected to his memory and this still stands at the kennels of the Cheshire Hunt at Sandiway. It is inscribed:

> In the memory of Bluecap, a foxhound,
> The late property of the Honble John Smith-Barry.
> If fame, honour and glory depend on the deed
> Then O Bluecap, rare Bluecap, we'll boast of thy breed.

It is now two hundred years since Bluecap died. Tales are told and his name is perpetuated at the Bluecap Hotel at Sandiway.

So are the names of the horses 'Spinner' and 'Bergamot' at Comberbach, though history records that 'Marbury Dunn' was the most noble horse of the Marbury stud, as supreme as was Bluecap at the kennels. There is no doubt that the quality and successes of horses and hounds of Marbury gave the Smith-Barrys prominence. Throughout the land great sporting occasions filled in the lives of the aristocracy in those days and gambling played a major part. Perhaps the most frequently told story of Marbury Dunn concerns his running from Charing Cross, London to Marbury Hall (180 miles) between the hours of sunrise and sunset on two consecutive days. Arriving at Marbury, allowed to drink water ad lib, he fell down and died. There was a plaque over his grave:

'Marbury Dunn – the finest horse that ever run.'

Also, when I looked back, I thought of two short stories perhaps you would like. The first of them is about a Girls' Friendly Society Concert held in the School. The first item was a song given by George Curbishley and Alfred Leigh, both of Aston. It was entitled 'Paddy MaGinty' and the first verse was:

Paddy MaGinty an Irishman of note
He came into a fortune and bought himself a goat
Said he of milk, I sure will have my fill
But when he got the Nanny home he found it was a Bill.

Shrieks and consternation of course! The only verse any of the girls could remember. Nice girls they were though. Very nice.

One Sunday Padre Smithett was in the pulpit delivering a sermon and pronounced, *"And the Lord said* (hearing a laugh from the choir he turned round and continued) *Kenneth Birtles go to the vestry at once."* Now, as to whether Kenneth went on instructions from Padre Smithett or from the Lord Himself I do not know – your guess is as good as mine. Kenneth himself said he was not sure.

Putting frivolity aside I will return to the story of the once-upon-a-time village band and to my wonder as to what had become of the instruments. Could they be among the many things dumped on the upper floor of the Reading Room? Well, along with a friend I have investigated and, lo and behold, we found two, just two. What became of the others we do not know. Now I have no knowledge as to the worth of such instruments but think they could be quite valuable, either for use, for sale or, best of all, for exhibition in the village or a local museum. I have no wish at all to trespass into the concert of others and have no such intention but I do feel justified in saying what a pity it is that so much is dumped up there. No doubt a lot of it is trifling – piles of crockery, clothing, cases of towelling and linens, old chairs and the like – but there are worthwhile articles. There are mementos, souvenirs, a dozen or so clean sound nursery chairs, two Singer sewing machines in cases, each around one hundred years old – what would they fetch at Sothebys? – and various other items. Most of all though I think of the room itself. I remember it as a very successful Village Club with a three-quarter-size billiards table. We played cards, darts, dominoes, etc – open every night except Sundays and it was a meeting room for various committees. Has this room, part of a building on which there is a preservation order, right in the centre, nothing to contribute to the life of the village of Great Budworth?

Enid Kelly

Enid Kelly was born at the Ring o' Bells, 50 Church Street, Great Budworth in 1919 as Enid Hubbard. The Hubbard family was a large family in Great Budworth in the early 1900s. She spent most of her life in the village shop (except for a period during the war when she was a Red Cross nurse at Arley) until the shop closed in 1978. As such, Enid has an unique perspective of village life. In addition, she has an excellent sense of humour, as can be appreciated by the following memory.

The Editors

Mrs Jenny Hubbard with daughter Enid Kelly and granddaughter Jane in village shop in 1968

Memories of Great Budworth ~ ~ Enid Kelly

This is the story of the lives of my grandparents and parents as told to me over the years. Also the story of my life.

My paternal grandfather Frank Hubbard was born in 1856 in Haddeston in Buckinghamshire. When he was about 18 he came to Cheshire looking for work. He walked all the way from Oxfordshire and found work at the salt works in Marston, the next village to Great Budworth. He met my grandmother, Sarah Astles, who was born in 1859 and was a Budworth girl. After they were married they lived first in Brownslow Cottages, Warrington Road, and then at 27 Southbank. They had 11 children William (known as Tom), Mary (Polly), Annie, Richard (Dick), Henry (Victor), Frederick, Gilbert, Frank, Roger, Connie and Clifford. Frederick, the middle one of the 11, was my father and he was born in 1890.

The Hubbard Family, circa 1900.   (Note: Clifford was born afterwards)
Back row: Frederick, Tom, Annie, Dick, Polly, Victor
Seated: Frank (on knee), Frank (father), Sarah (mother), Connie (on knee)
Front row: Gilbert and Roger

Times were very hard and Dad remembers as a child taking babies as they came along to his mother who was working in the fields to be breast fed. It wasn't until the older ones in the family, Polly, Tommy and Annie started working and were able to help out that things were a little easier.

95

Father was quite a good scholar, the school master took a special interest in him and about four other boys in his class, who showed more promise than the rest of the class and approached his father about dad going in for teaching. Dad though, at the early age of about eleven was showing signs of deafness and in those days it was a great drawback. As it was he went four nights week to the next village, Marston, to night school - two miles away. This cost twopence a night and they had to supply their own books, which was considered quite expensive. He was always grateful to his elder brother Tom for paying for this extra education. I remember him once saying that each time he paid for Uncle Tom a 'pint' he was paying off a bit of his back debt.

Father's first job was on a farm, but he didn't stay long as he had the chance of working at South Bank House, near his home, as a coachman, to a Mrs Egerton-Warburton. He enjoyed that as he had a smart uniform, one of the 'perks' of the job. He tells of taking Mrs Warburton out for afternoon tea to big houses as far as eight or ten miles away. This took a couple of hours to get there, about an hour and a half for the tea, and the trip back, so nearly a day out just for afternoon tea. He says that at the time he only had 'working' clothes and his livery uniform, so on Sunday he had to stay home as he hadn't got a best suit, so he couldn't even go to Church, although he had joined the choir at the age of seven.

When he first joined the choir, he tells of the very cold night when he decided to sit on some warm pipes at the back of the choir stalls and fell asleep. When he woke up, at about one o'clock in the morning - the moon was shining through the stained-glass windows. He started screaming and banging on the locked door, but not until the local Doctor, coming back from a sick patient at five in the morning, heard this noise and went for the sexton did he manage to get out. His mother had never missed him, I suppose with a family that size it could easily happen. Dad never forgot the feeling of horror, he had no voice left, with shouting, for days.

After working at Mrs Warburton's for a year or two, he started working in Arley gardens and so started his life as a gardener, which he was for the rest of his working days. When he first started at Arley he walked there and back until he managed to save 12s 6d for his first bicycle. From Arley he went to work at Sandicroft, this was about 1913, and is where mother appeared on the scene, so now over to mother's beginnings.

Mother was one of nine children born to Ralph and Annie Boyd in Northumberland. (Her mother, my grandmother, was born at a Pub called the Hope and Anchor, which is still there.) Mother's father died when the eldest child was about 15yrs, so her mother was left to bring up this large family on her own. While their father was alive, things weren't too bad as he was a master cabinet maker, but after he died things were terribly hard. My grandmother did all kinds of work to help feed the family. She made bread which mother had to deliver before she went to school, also granny took in washing and did decorating for neighbours. Her main job though, was delivering babies and laying out the dead. A job which she didn't mind, as, if they couldn't afford to pay, she always got a 'drop' of whisky, which I must add was one of her weaknesses.

Back to mother, when she was about ten years old she went to live with an aunt and uncle, and even though they were marvellous to her, she was very homesick for her brothers and sisters, so she went home.

When she left school, she went into service to be a kitchen maid, where her maiden Aunt Kate, was cook and later became Housekeeper at this house called Dalmaire. Mother didn't get home for two years, as this Aunt Kate made her send all her wages home to her mother, which must have been very tough for a young girl, especially as she was very homesick still. Mother says even though she thought it terrible at the time, she's always been grateful for the training she had there. The people were very good living people and were very good to the staff. She loved wearing a long dress and her hair 'up' for prayers at night, which she looked forward to all day.

From there, mother went to work in Newcastle to be nearer home, for a family called Renwick. While working there this family decided to move into Cheshire, in fact to Sandicroft in Great Budworth. They wanted mother to move with them, but she didn't want to leave the 'North.' So she said that she would come for a fortnight to help them move in. This was in 1914 and while she was in Cheshire the war started. Mrs Renwick, asked her to stay longer to help with her seven year old boy. Her husband had joined the army and immediately became Major Renwick. This is how my mother and father met. The major went straight out to France and Mrs Renwick wanted to join him. She called mother and father into the drawing room one morning and suggested that they got married as she didn't like leaving mother in such a large house with only a child as company. Dad said he didn't mind if Jenny didn't and mother said she didn't mind. So that's how they came to get married. That was on April 21st 1915.

97

'Twopence to spend'
Village Shop, 50 Church Street, circa 1936

Dad and three of his brothers joined the army in 1914 on the same day. How awful for Granny Hubbard to have four of her sons walk out of the house like that. Dad was only in four months, he had managed to disguise his deafness at his medical test, but he was sent home after this short spell. Frank and Roger were both wounded and Henry was killed, getting the DCM for bravery.

By this time father thought they ought to have a home of their own. The only empty one at the time was 50 Church Street, the one in which they spent the next 60 years. Mother said it nearly broke her heart when she saw it for the first time - she swore they had kept hens upstairs, it was so dirty. It had originally been a pub called the Ring o' Bells, then a farm and a shop. My mother's eldest sister Cissy and Samuel Hunt had a shop in Manchester. So at Sam's suggestion they decided to reopen the shop - so started a business. Uncle Sam lent them £40 to start off with and I still have the letter that Dad wrote thanking him for the loan and paying the last of this £40 off. It is written on black-edged paper and states that as he has killed off two pigs and sold them he's able to finish off the loan. (I presume that the black-edged paper is because of the death of the pigs.)

It is fitting that when we sold the house many years later it was bought by Samuel Hunt's son, Bert Hunt.

Father also had two fields and a couple of horses so, on top of his gardening job, they must have worked from morning until night. Even though they worked so hard, they were still 'hard up', trying to get the house furnished and buying stock for the small-holding etc. In those days they had lots of bad debts.

Dad used to make black puddings and brawn when he killed a pig to sell in the shop, nothing was wasted.

At one time they started to make fish and chips, this was quite a success, until one night the fish kettle (a very large pan with a handle at both sides) caught fire. Dad and his brother Gilbert put a brush handle through the handles of the pan and carried it out into the middle of the yard. Dad says the flames were fierce and all the youths in the village were looking over the yard wall, shouting *"Eh up there's Hubbard's shit tin's on fire."* So ended the chip shop.

By this time they had bought a small 'trap,' so with this they did a bit of 'transport' work, taking people back and to from the station and into Northwich, etc. That didn't last long as mother got the horse into a gallop. Then she tried to pull up too sharp and the poor horse fell to its knees and so broke the shafts of the trap, so another idea came to a stop.

Shortly after the Rev Smithett moved into the village he met three girls and asked them their names. The first was my sister Connie, she curtsied and said *"my name is Constance Hubbard"*, then Florrie said *"my name is Florence Dickens"*, finally Mary not to be outdone by her friends said her name was Marence Dickens.

The house as I got older, always seemed to be full of visitors. My Aunty Maggie's family from Manchester, there were eight of them, spent the school holidays here, usually two at a time. It was mother's idea of giving her sister a rest. Ernest the eldest was always popular, as he was the same age as my eldest brother Frank. Ernie tells the tale of 'larking' about next door with the son at The George and Dragon. As Mrs Bell the owner was out, the lads decided to give the pigs all the dregs out of the beer barrels. When Mrs Bell came home, the pigs were all lying around the pub yard - dead drunk.

I must go back to my grandparents, dad's family. My grandfather and I shared the same birthday, December 23rd. I remember when I was six or seven, him saying to me it wasn't fair him being so old and me so young and yet we had the same birthday. It took me quite a while to work that one out. He was a lovely old man, very like my father in looks. Funny, as a child it always seemed to be summer. He had a summer house at the bottom of their garden, looking over both meres. Every night he would send up to the George and Dragon for a jug of beer. There would be three or four of the grandchildren sitting with him and we all had to have a taste of the beer straight from the jug. I remember Wilfred one of the 'lads' knocking this jug over and breaking it. Of course he had to have a new jug, but I always remember thinking the beer never tasted quite the same out of the new one. I don't remember my Granny Hubbard too well, only that she was very slight and a bit severe. Dad said that she wasn't at all like that, so I think she must have been ill then. She died when she was 72, grandad was 80.

He used to come up to our house every Sunday morning - in the summer he would have a beer and in the colder winter he would have a glass of Port or home-made wine. He was always very smart in grey, with a nice grey trilby and a silver topped walking stick.

Five of the family lived to be over 80 years, Dad and Sam over 90 years. Father died March 9th 1980, a month before their 65th wedding anniversary. Mother died July 1st 1982, after an illness of 4 years, after having a stroke. My Aunty Connie died in 1983 after a short illness.

I'll always be grateful for the happy childhood my parents made for my three brothers and myself and the way they both worked for us.

My eldest brother was born at Sandicroft on March 7th 1916. I was born in 50 Church Street in 1919. My younger brother, Jack was born in 1921 and my youngest brother Frederick in 1933.

I went to school at Great Budworth school until I was 14. After school I worked in my mother's shop until the war broke out in 1940. Throughout the war I worked for the Red Cross at Arley Hall. At first we were looking after children evacuated from London, but later in the war we were looking after wounded soldiers. There were up to 30 wounded soldiers recouperating at Arley Hall at any one time.

In 1940 I met Ambrose Kelly and we were married in 1942. Ambrose was serving in the Royal Navy, so we only saw each other when he was on leave.

34 School Lane

In 1944 we moved to 34 School Lane for which we paid £5 3s per annum rent. In 1948 we bought this cottage for £130.

We had four children - Peter, John, Paul and Jane. Three boys and a girl was exactly the same as my mother had had years earlier.

I always worked in the village shop with my mother and father. When the houses were built in Westage Lane in 1952 we moved there from School Lane.

When my mother and father retired from the shop we exchanged houses.

Finally, when Ambrose retired in 1978, we moved into my mother's house in Westage Lane and the village shop closed after 60 years. It was with great regret that we had to close the shop but we could no longer compete with the supermarkets. The shop holds many happy memories it was a great joy talking and meeting all the villagers.

Enid Kelly on her last day at the shop.

Before I close I have been persuaded to recount a few of the many stories which have made my life so enjoyable.

During the War, when I was a nurse at Arley, there was a worldly nurse working with me. Working in the village shop I knew little of such things. One day when we were having a cup of tea and talking about our boy friends she said in a very posh accent, *"Enid do you believe in free love?"*

In my naivety I replied, *"Of course I do, he only gets eight bob a day and he spends most of that on baccy."*

Around the time of decimalisation one posh lady came into the shop and I said that the change was 50p. The customer said, *"I won't use that vulgar term, I shall still call them pence".*

Then Lil Baker came in and I asked her if she would use the term pence or pee.

She replied, *"Indeed not I'll call it by its proper name, piss".*

A village character who was very rotund came into the shop one day with his flies open. I told him and said he had better do them up.

The corpulant customer, who shall remain nameless, replied, *"No love, you do them, you're much nearer than me."*

Memories of Great Budworth ~ ~ Enid Kelly

The Running Pump, Great Budwoth

103

Roger Wilkinson

Roger Wilkinson was not born in Great Budworth but nonetheless he is so well-known in mid Cheshire, that if any one deserves the title 'Mr Budworth' it is Roger Wilkinson. He has spent over 50 years farming in Great Budworth and has seen the change from horse-drawn ploughs to the mechanised business which is farming today. In addition, for many years he served on the NFU Council, on Great Budworth Parish Council for 27 years and on Runcorn Rural District Council. He probably rates his favourite achievement as the resurrection of the bowling green from a derelict lorry park to the asset to the Great Budworth community it is today.

The Editors

Roger Wilkinson about 1965

My name is Roger Wilkinson and I was born in Grappenhall on 10 January 1917. I have lived, worked and farmed in the area all that time so it is hardly any wonder I have seen quite a few changes in the methods of farming and the habits of farmers during the twentieth century. I came to Great Budworth as a tenant farmer of the Arley Estate to White Hart Farm in High Street in February 1945. At that time there were four farms within the village – all approximately 40 to 50 acres and within 100 yards of the Lych Gate. Mr Fred Renshaw, who farmed Saracen's Head, was completely arable and had no livestock at all but the other three all carried a milking herd.

Goldmine Farm was Mr Tom Howard's - he milked cows and was a mixed dairy farmer - and Henry Jones who lived at Westage Farm in Westage Lane used the buildings at Hough Farm for his milking herd.

I farmed White Hart Farm, which was 45 acres, and milked 16 cows, kept a few hens and some pigs. The farm buildings adjoined the farm house which is now White Hart Barn - you didn't need central heating when you had cattle the other side of the kitchen wall. This shippon housed 8 cows and had a loft over where we kept all the potato sets for the following year. Generally, most farms had a crop rotation of 5 years: two years grass, one year potatoes, one year wheat and one year oats and most farms had a little bit of everything with a few hens, and a pig here or there.

When I moved to Great Budworth there were no tractors on any of the farms, every farm carried two or maybe three horses who did all the ploughing and cultivation plus all the harvesting and carting of the corn by horse and cart. There was no stable at White Hart so I stabled my horses at Duncalf's where Norman Duncalf now lives at 59 High Street. This was also by an arrangement through Arley Estate and Mr Duncalf, who was also a tenant of Arley's at that time.

Going back to the dairy herd, the cows from White Hart were driven through Church Street and down through Westage Lane in the summer every morning and brought back for milking each evening. After evening milking they would graze one of the fields we had behind the farm which ran down to the main road and around to the running pump. Incidentally, at that time Hillybank (as we called it) was completely free of trees and the cows grazed the bank. It just goes to show what would happen if land was not touched for a few years without any farming on it.

The land was split up into many, many little fields. Mr Jones from Hough Farm andWestage Farm had the land down Smithy Lane and right up the Butts. Saracen's Head had a belt of land right from Westage Lane up the middle and through to Quebec Wood. White Hart had two fields up Heath Lane but the bulk was on the east side of Heath Lane running up to the Sandhole, called Westage. Mr Jones also had two fields by the Sandhole off Westage Lane. Goldmine Farm's fields were behind the Church on the bank.

When I moved to Great Budworth there were no houses beyond Smithy Cottage and Cob Cottage either side of Westage Lane until you came to Farthings Lane where there was a small thatched cottage and also Westage Farm where Mr Jones lived.

105

To give you some idea, all the fields down there were in three- or four-acre fields with hedges dividing them up. Mr Jones also had cows which travelled up Church Street, down the Butts and sometimes along Westage Lane to his place at Westage Farm.

The corn in those days was harvested with a binder and set up in stooks on the fields for two to three weeks until the corn had ripened and then it was carted by horse and cart to various points in the village. Renshaws came down by Southbank, around behind the Vicarage and he had two or three stacks made at the bottom of Saracen's Head where he had a stackyard.

During the winter we would get the Threshing Machine to the village to thresh the corn. This was pulled by a twelve-ton steam engine pulling the four-ton thresher and the bale press which must also have weighed approximately four tons - twenty tons in total weight. The engine driver would negotiate going down Southbank, under the archway to Tom Howard's stacks or around to Mr Renshaw's at Saracen's Head. Mr Renshaw also had some land up the lane by the Old Hall where he would invariably have one or two stacks, so the thresher would be taken up there and it would leave a trail of dust wherever it went. I cannot remember anyone complaining but villagers would brush up the dust trail. Cows would often lick the windows as they passed or leave a few droppings in the street but again no-one complained - it was probably used for the vegetable garden.

As far as labour was concerned there were always boys from the school (they stayed at the village school until they were fourteen in those days) who were willing to give you a hand on the farm. It seemed to me that folk who lived in Great Budworth prior to the depression of the early thirties were predominantly agricultural workers, so their offspring were very farm orientated and you could always get men who had moved on to ICI or the Salt Works as shift workers to come and give you a hand at busy times. Incidentally, they knew how the work was done and didn't need any instruction from me. This was a great asset at harvest and potato picking time.

As far as the fields are concerned, in 1954 Arley Estate decided to sell White Hart Farm and build another holding up Heath Lane, where we already had a two-bay shed. This was called New Westage Farm. Mr Henry Jones decided to leave Hough Farm buildings and Westage Farm so both of these were sold as private dwellings and the land was put on to New Westage Farm where I was. The same thing happened a few years later when Mr Renshaw retired so three farms went to make New Westage Farm.

This enlargement of farms has been going on for many years and, as far as making fields bigger, this was the policy of the Government of the day. There was a need to feed the nation, food was rationed, as was fuel and clothing, so necessity became the mother of invention and the age of the tractors and contract work meant fields became bigger and farming progressed to provide a staple diet for all.

I will go back now to the time I took over the tenancy of White Hart Farm from Mr John Mosley who was a widower and who, at that time, had five sons and a daughter. One son had left school and the others weren't far behind so he took a bigger farm at Hulme Hall, Allostock. John Mosley had grown a lot of potatoes during the war which was a general trend to feed folk so half the farm was cows and half potatoes. He also had a milk retail licence and the question was, do I keep it on? I did.

I bought my first cow to provide certain customers who came each morning, to our door, for their milk. We also kept a few hens, so eggs and milk were sold at the door by the jugful and in June there was a great trade for early new potatoes. There was always a great race to produce the first potatoes and we would be running to and fro from the field picking them really fresh. The locals liked their potatoes fresh, nobody wanted stale spuds, they wouldn't have them, they knew better.

When we got milking in a bigger way, as we could afford to buy more cows, we sent our surplus milk to the milk board and it was picked up each day at 8 am. The milk wagon came up the hill and picked the milk tankards up on the street in front of White Hart. The carrier was always H B Corker of Lostock who took the milk off to Manchester.

Everyone had a similar practice of farming except at one time we were enticed into growing peas for Pickerings. They had to be carted when they were ready to a vinery at Georges Lane, Aston Budworth. This didn't last long as Pickerings sold out to Fisons who cleared off to Lincoln which was a bigger area with bigger fields. It was a short-lived but lucrative time - we nicknamed the peas Pickerings Cannonballs!! Peas were a great crop-breaker because overgrowing of potatoes on the same land for too long meant we had an infestation of eel worm so peas helped to rid us of this.

A little about village life. The traffic problem was very different with only about six of us having a car but the bus service was very regular. Buses came to the village each day, and on Fridays and Saturdays each hour, taking folk to Northwich to do their shopping. This made a big difference to how people got around.

We used to run Whist Drives and a big one which I had the pleasure of 'MC'ing for many years was a feathered Whist Drive at Christmas for the Church, yes you've guessed it - prizes were dead turkeys, geese, ducks and chickens in the feather! We even had rabbits too (this made it a fur and feather Whist Drive). We had up to 40 tables in the school which involved a lot of carting tables and chairs around so eventually, after many years, we moved the whole issue to Antrobus Village Hall but it was still held for our Church. This was in the days of Canon Foster.

Parish Councils and District Councils were elected in a different way - no secret ballot. An open meeting would be held in the school and anyone wanting to put up for Parish or District had to submit their name. It was done by a show of hands there and then. You had to stand up and be counted which was sometimes a bit embarrassing. I always remember in my first year in the village Fred Renshaw was the Clerk of the Council and there was an election for the District Councillor.

Roger Wilkinson ploughing with two horses, circa 1948

A well-known figure in the village, Mr Harry Walton, a man I knew very well before I came to the village, was District Councillor on Runcorn Rural Council for many years but a local farmer, Mr George Hewitt, of Cock Lane Farm, was putting up to oppose him. According to the rules an independent person had to take the Chair. Mr Renshaw asked me but little did I know what was going on, or who was putting up. It was very embarrassing when Harry Walton was defeated by George Hewitt and I had to declare the number of votes. Being a newcomer to the village I was exceedingly nervous.

There were a lot of people who came to White Hart each morning with their jugs for fresh milk and, living at the front of the house, you could see many comings and goings on the High Street. In the evenings people would pass on their way to the George & Dragon. One dear old lady, Mrs Hughes, went up each evening at 8 pm with her shawl around her head to get a pint of mild to take back to her husband. Harry Walton passed each morning going down to the tailor's shop with his tape measure draped around his neck.

People came to the door for potatoes and we made lots of friends who gave us advice about living on a street which we had never done before, but we got used to it eventually.

The condition of the houses was totally different from today's standards. Electricity was downstairs only, candles upstairs, no toilets in the house but a bucket closet down the yard past the piggeries - a very big change in 50 years.

Various people helped us on the farm for casual work. Mr Bill Martin and his family helped. Bill worked as a shift man at ICI and I knew his shifts nearly as well as he did so he could always help me when he was off. Mr Ted Dickens also helped quite a lot and the Billingtons from the top of the hill. None of these men needed any training.

Probably before I finish I should record the history of the Parish Hall and Bowling Green in Smithy Lane. The ground was given by the Arley Estate, just after the First World War, as a memorial to the people who had served their country. A Bowling Green was established on the land, most probably with a good deal of voluntary help, and this was opened in 1920 and continued as a popular village amenity but it fell into disrepair after the outbreak of the Second World War in 1939. When I moved to the village in 1945 it was overgrown - a good yard high - and was used as a cycle track. In fact I grazed calves on it for a few years.

The land and the old Smithy were given to the Parish with Trustees, Dr Gilbert Love, Mr Harry Walton and the Vicar in charge. In 1959 the Trustees decided it was fitting for the Parish Council to control the running of the Hall (Smithy) and Bowling Green as opposed to Trustees. At that time I was Chairman of the Parish Council and we managed to obtain grants and we made the Smithy into a useable Parish Hall. The Bowling Green was by now a lorry park and also the venue for the annual bonfire so we had many meetings to decide possible uses. Some thought a car park would be a village asset but it was decided to re-instate it as a Bowling Green. The Green opened in 1972 after a great deal of voluntary help and in 1974 a pavilion was built by Jim Huddleston and other volunteers using second-hand materials and this was opened in 1975. The Parish Hall has taken great strides, has recently been renovated and enlarged. It supplies the village community with all its needs and was re-opened in 1996. It is a credit to all the hard work put in by so many villagers to take Great Budworth Parish Hall into the 21st century.

The village can be most indebted to the owners of the Arley Estate for the way they have treated Budworth as their village prior to selling it in 1948 and they have continued their interest in Great Budworth right up to this present day.

Roger Wilkinson   9th August 1999

The Wilkinson family at harvest time, circa 1980
Left to right: Roger, Stephen, Peter, Bob and David

Left to right: Fred Hubbard, Mary Scott and Roger Wilkinson
planting a tree to celebrate the Queen's Silver Jubilee
in 1977.

Annie Littler

Mrs Annie Littler - the lady with the round shiny face, always busy. She is a great gardener, cook and knitter. At the age of 89 she is still to be found in her garden digging when the weather allows. If the weather is bad she is busy crocheting or knitting. If this is not enough, she also cleans the bottom pump house. She gives a constant amount of her woolly goods to the village fair held every November. She now belongs to a day centre and that too sees the fruits of her labour. She is a great baker - every Christmas she bakes at least twenty cakes for friends and relatives. She is much in demand to do teas for the various societies. People have fond memories also of her little poodles Savu and Ponsu who used to go to the Post Office every day to pick up their daily bars of chocolate.

The Editors

Annie Littler and Ponsu

My name is Annie Littler and I was born on 1st April 1911 in Chesterfield, Derbyshire, being christened at the church with the crooked spire.

In 1929, I acquired the job as scullery maid at Tabley House, Knutsford. My parents put me on the train at Staveley to go via Manchester and Altrincham then finally to Knutsford. Due to a wrong connection the chauffeur had given me up at Knutsford, but a kindly railway porter persuaded the chauffeur to return. Thus commenced my 40 years of service in various Cheshire households - Tabley being the grandest. Captain and Mrs Leicester Warren and their two children resided at Tabley. The staff was pretty vast but the family entertained a lot and were most hospitable. The internal staff comprised a housekeeper, lady's maid, butler, two footmen, hallboy, three housemaids, cook, kitchen maid, scullery maid and dairy maid. I slept with two other maids over the kitchen. Life though long and hard was full of fun. In the evenings the servants used to play games, have singsongs, listen to the wireless, etc. in the servants' hall. Males and females of the lower order were not allowed to be together unless chaperoned by a more senior member of staff. We were paid the handsome amount of £2 a month in 1930.

During my time there, the fabric of the chapel was moved brick by brick from the island in the large lake to its present position. Bishop Paget of Chester re-dedicated the chapel which was a historic occasion.

My strong connection with the village of Great Budworth commenced with the arrival at Tabley Hall of Sam Littler. Sam Littler was born at Brownslow Farm Cottage, Warrington Road in September 1901. His father, also Sam, worked at Brownslow Farm which in those days was a stud farm. They then moved to Clock Cottage, Westage Lane which was then two cottages, where Sam Senior worked at Aston Park. The next move was to Hilltop Cottage where Sam Senior worked for the Gibbon family at Hilltop Farm. This small cottage housed nine children: Sam, Jack, Tom, Joe, Annie, Jessie, Lucy, Maggie and Olive. All the children went to Great Budworth School. Sam junior took a particular interest in gardening. People from Reaseheath came regularly to the school to teach gardening on an allotment down School Lane. Sam Junior got a job helping at Arley Gardens. It was here he learned to plough and Sam and his brothers helped to install the bowling green in the village of Great Budworth. Unfortunately, having worked hard on the green, on completion they were told they couldn't join the bowling club as they were not parishioners - Hilltop Cottage being in Aston-by-Budworth and not Great Budworth.

Courtship between two employees was not permitted in those days so reluctantly I found live-in employment at Stockton Heath. We used to meet regularly at Sam's parents' home, both cycling the respective distances. I then moved to work at the Vicarage, Lostock Gralam, where Sam was allowed to visit me. We finally got married in Great Budworth Church on 15th June 1932.

Married life started at Tabley Brook Cottage and I was re-employed as cook at Tabley House. We enjoyed our cycle ride to work. In those days the A556 was very quiet except when Blackpool Illuminations were on. We saw the road widened twice. When the Leicester Warrens went visiting, Sam and I moved into the staff wing to supervise the house and the junior staff. War put an end to our convivial life at Tabley House. Sam had to change from horticulture to agriculture and worked for Mr and Mrs Gibbon who had moved to farm at Marston. In those days there were three cottages at the entrance to the farm called Bullbarn Cottages. We moved into one of them and I worked at ICI Winnington cleaning out the lime kilns. Sam's parents now lived at Hough Farm, Church Street, and we regularly cycled and walked around the area. I remember filling up sand bags at the sandpit outside the village for sand bag bunkers.

At the end of the war Sam finished farming at Marston and we both moved to Dene House. I was companion to Mrs Robinson who was a semi-invalid and Sam gardened. The Robinsons were delightful. Their business was a storage warehouse in Manchester. We lived with them for 7 or 8 years. Besides being a companion, we soon acquired some livestock. Sam milked the cow, we raised and dressed poultry. I made butter, cheese and did a lot of baking. These offerings were given away as gifts. During this time we joined in the local Budworth activities. A cricket pitch was set up at Dene House and the men used to play. Providence House was rented by Doctor Love and the main room was used for 'Saturday Hops' which cost sixpence. The WI also met there and we had film shows. Dr Love's chauffeur and family, the Shinglers, were residents of this house. Providence Cottage was a tearoom run by Mrs Hart. At weekends the walls along Church Street were propped up with many bicycles. Church was also a focal point of our lives.

In those days there were not any main drains. Some fortunate houses had a septic tank or had a large garden where a pit was dug. A vivid memory is of the householders wheeling their buckets in a barrow up past the church early on Sunday morning to tip their human waste at the sand pit on the other side of the village.

These post-war days were happy ones. I got involved in the Christmas fairs to raise money for the village hall - the Old Smithy. Several improvements were done over the years.

In 1948 the big auction took place. We acquired No 7 and No 8 The Mount for £400. Miss Mellor stayed in No 7 as a sitting tenant until her death. Maggie Littler moved into No 8. It was not until Sam's retirement in 1968 that we finally moved into our house - No 7.

Unfortunately the Robinsons moved out of Dene House in 1953 and we were jobless. Miss Esmé Love, in the village, had been collecting money for the coronation celebrations. We moved to employment in Tarporley before the big event. We watched the coronation on a television and cycled to Great Budworth for a meal in the school. Cycling to Great Budworth was a long way with no suitable buses, so we then went to work at an old people's home at Bowdon. This was more convenient as the bus took us as far as Pickmere and then we could walk.

Our final employment was with Mr & Mrs Chippendale near to the now M56. We lived in a flat over the garage and since our employers were away a great deal, life was easy. Sam also had use of a car. However, in 1968 we both retired and took possession of our Budworth home.

Len Martin

Len Martin was born in Great Budworth to Bill and Florrie Martin and was one of six children who were born and brought up in 36 School Lane. This house was described in the 1948 sale catalogue as 'Living Room, Scullery, 2 Bedrooms, Outside Washhouse and Earth Closet'. The annual rent was £4 10s. Today it is difficult to imagine how a family of eight could live in such a small house but that was typical of many of the cottages in Budworth at that time. There were some cottages which were even more crowded. However, the Martins were obviously a happy family despite their hardship. The Martin family are synonymous with Great Budworth in the inter-war years. Len's father Bill Martin was a great character. Like his father, Len worked at I.C.I. and now lives in Antrobus but still has a great affection for Great Budworth.

The Editors

Back row: Tony Martin, Donald Reay, Austin Hughes,
David Eaton, Len Martin
Front row: Matty Moores, Donald Rose

My name is Len Martin and I was born at 36 School Lane, Great Budworth on 10 March 1930, the third son of Bill and Florence. There were 6 children – 4 boys and 2 girls. We were brought up in a small two up and two down cottage with no hot water or flush toilets.

Monday was always wash day and our wash house was across the cobblestone yard with a coal boiler and a big wooden mangle. When the washing was finished, the boiler was filled again for us all to have a bath. We hated being the last one in the bath because the water had gone cold and was murky. It was also very cold in the winter. The lavatory was also across the yard.

We lived mainly on potatoes, bread and rabbits. We also had plenty of vegetables which my father grew in his garden. All the cooking was done on a coal-fired oven. The tennis court is now where our garden was. We had our first wireless in 1939.

Water was not laid on until 1935-6 so our water supply came from the village tap in the pump house. There were 5 pumps in the village made of cast iron, weighing about 5 cwt. each. These were taken for scrap during the Second World War, together with all metal fences and gates.

The water for these pumps came from the meadows down the avenue. There was a ram pump which pumped the water to a big tank in the garden of Providence House. The pumps were situated by the bowling green, the pump house, South Bank, opposite the Post Office and on The Mount. Dene House was supplied with water from the same spring as the running pump at the bottom of the Dene. This was pumped by a ram pump on the bank along the main road which is in a big cellar. Every Saturday morning a man from Dene House used to oil and clean it. We, as young lads, used to wait for him to open the trap door and go down. We would then lock him in and would then toss up who would let him out because he was 6ft 6in tall and could stride over the black and white railings and catch us.

I started school at the age of four and my teacher was Miss Poole. In the winter we had Horlicks made in a big urn with a plunger. There was a big coal fire which the teacher always stood in front of. The nit nurse used to come on a regular basis to inspect us for head lice and also the dentist with his treadle drill and pliers. When I moved into the next class Miss Owen was our teacher and she would take us on lots of nature study walks. She was also a great lover of music and I think that is how I got my love of music. There was a maypole in the playground and on Empire Day we would dress up and parade.

The top class was taught by the headmaster, Ernest Southern (Scutcher). He was called this because if we misbehaved he would say, *"Go to the school field and cut a nice hazel stick."* He would then hit us all over with it. He liked the lads to be good gardeners and we went into the school garden two or three times a week. The war was on now and all the older lads (12 upwards) had special cards for farm work. We were only supposed to go so many half days a year but the farmers were always coming to school for us. I did very little schooling from the age of 12. The school leaving age was 14 then.

On a Sunday we went to Sunday School and my first teacher was Miss Hughes who lived at Royal Oak Cottage in Aston-by-Budworth. We were in Sunday School for an hour and then went into Church by the back door and sat behind the choir. We came out when the sermon started. As we got older we had to go in the afternoon as well and I joined the choir at the age of 7. There were about 18 boys and 10 men in the choir then. Mr Smith (Dido) was the organist and one Sunday during the sermon he fell asleep and tumbled off the organ seat. The boys couldn't sing for laughing. We used to take it in turns to pump the organ and at the end of the service we used to fill the bellows and run out of church, much to the annoyance of Dido.

Sometimes Mr Brasnett, the vicar, would take 5 or 6 boys to sing at Arley Chapel in his Flying Standard. If it was chestnut time he had a job to get us in the chapel. We went to church three times each Sunday. During the war the soldiers from Marbury Camp came once a month and the church would be full. As a treat, the vicar would let us go up the tower two or three times a year. The lads made paper aeroplanes and parachutes and the village would be covered in them. There was always a Sunday School trip once a year either to Blackpool or New Brighton and we also had a party in the school.

Whenever there was a party, dance or social in the school the Martin lads used to carry 100 heavy wooden chairs from Providence House to the school and then we had to carry the parish crockery from the cellar of the old vicarage. Sometimes Dr Frazer would show us his magic lantern. Dr Frazer worked with Dr Love until he joined the army.

There was also a big fete once a year at Belmont Park. We would all walk from the village in procession and it was a great day. We had our tea in the servants' quarters at the Hall.

The sexton at the Church was Mr Cocksey who was a very gifted man. He was a very good stone mason and carved gravestones. His workshop was the hest house which was opposite the old schoolroom. It was called the hest house because that is where the hearse was kept.

There were four working farms in the village. Fred Renshaw lived at Saracen's Head. John Mosley farmed White Hart which was later owned by Roger Wilkinson. Tom Howard lived at Gold Mine and Henry Jones at Westage Farm, which was known as Bale Wire Farm. The reason for this was because if any implement broke it was always mended with bale wire. There were two milking herds in the village. All the cows walked through the village twice a day for milking and all corn, potatoes, cattle fodder and manure came up and down the street on horse and cart.

In winter time the steam thresher came to thresh the corn which was great fun for the village lads. It was always know as the Jigger. We were paid 3 old pence an hour on the farms.

All our games were played at different seasons. Duck stone quack, marbles, top and whip, conkers, trundles, fox and hounds, football, cricket, rounders and fishing were our pastimes. Another thing all the village lads did was collect firewood because all the houses had open fires.

They all had nicknames and here are some of them: Wonkey Walker, Shinny Walker, Ferdy Hubbard, Huggy Hughes, Camel Hughes, Ciggy Eaton, Potty Eaton, Flomp Garner, Bown Martin, Toe Martin, Smiler Martin, Cog Dickens, Gover Scott, Jotter Thompson and Spadger Parry.

In 1948 Arley Estate sold the village and my father bought his house for £180.

36 School Lane, circa 1910

119

Mona Magnall

Peter Magnall answered an appeal for information on Great Budworth in 1999. Below is his covering note followed by Mona's memories. Sadly Mona died on 20th March 2000.

The Editors

My mother, Mona Magnall, formerly Scott, was born on 18th January 1907 and lived the first 22 years of her life at 32 School Lane, Great Budworth. These jottings are the result of conversations with her in her 93rd year, i.e. 1999 and some notes she wrote herself.

Peter Magnall

Mona Magnall

GREAT BUDWORTH PEOPLE

Mona's parents were James and Mary Scott and they raised their family of eight children in 32 School Lane, which had formerly been the home of James's parents, John and Martha Scott and their family.

The cottage was the property of the Warburton family who lived at Arley Hall. Tenants used to go to the Hall once a year to pay the rent and every tenant was given a piece of beef from one of the cattle bred on the Estate. In later years, instead of the beef the families were given a good meal at the Cock Hotel in Great Budworth.

Childhood is remembered as a happy time, a favourite play area being the meadows close to home. One memory is of having to carry all the drinking water from a tap at the end of the lane. In the summer, this would sometimes run dry and water would have to be carried from the ever-running pump at the bottom of the Dene Hill. This water source had been in use for many years and never known to run dry and the water was always cold.

When about 12 years old, during school holidays the children were allowed to help on the farm picking potatoes for which they were paid 2/6d a day for working from 8 am to 5 pm There was an hour for lunch and a mid-morning and afternoon break.

Mona's sister, Alice, who was 2 years older, joined the Land Army in the 1914-1918 war.

Particular friends of the Scott family were the Dickens family. When 14 years old mother was allowed to go to dances held in the School next door. These were very happy days.

32 School Lane

At 34 School Lane lived Violet and Dick Cocksey. Dick was a stone mason and also churchwarden. They had 2 children, Dorothy and William.

At 36 School Lane was Granny Cocksey, mother of Dick. She used to make nettle beer.

Mr and Mrs Ralph Platt lived at 38 School Lane. They had no children.

Living at 40 School Lane were James and Agnes Scott and their seven children. James was the son of Peter Scott and nephew to the above James Scott.

The schoolmaster occupied 30 School Lane. About 1913, this was Mr Sproston and he was succeeded by Mr Harry Smith. The clematis (Jackmoni), which until recently still grew by the bay window of the cottage, was there about 1913.

Dr Love, who came from Ireland, lived at the Manor House, next door (downhill) to the George & Dragon. Mrs Love's sister, Miss Muir also lived with them.

Dr. Love had a pony and trap, which was used to pay a weekly visit to Northwich on a Friday. One Friday they returned shortly after leaving, because Mrs Love had collapsed and died. Years later Dr. Love married Miss Muir, his sister-in-law.

Later, John Shingler was the chauffeur to old Dr Love. John lived at Providence House and had a son George. George was later the organist at the church for several years.

Gilbert Love eventually took over the practice and lived at the Old Hall. He and Mrs Love had two children; eldest was Peter and he had a sister Wendy.

Mr. Priestner, a farmer, bought the next house to Dr. Love (the elder) and had bay windows fitted.

Mrs Alice Hart lived next door to Providence House; she used to play the piano at some of the village social evenings.

Mr Bowden lived in the last cottage on the left of Church Street going out of the village. He had a housekeeper, Mrs Adair, widow of Mr Adair and from Germany.

Mr Blackstock and son Jim were blacksmiths and also ran the village Post Office.

Farmers in the immediate area included the Drinkwaters, John, Charles and sister Emily. John was sweet on Miss Graves, the schoolmistress, but she did not return his affection.

The Warburton family lived at South Bank House.

The Mount
Mr & Mrs J Lever - Sarah & John (last house on The Mount). John was in the Church choir.
Mr & Mrs Curbishley and family. Alice was one of the children and was at school with Mona Scott.
Mr & Mrs Eaton and family. Doris, one of the daughters worked at the tailors. Billy and Fred were the sons. Fred married Mary Dickens.

High Street
Mr & Mrs Thornton
Mrs Hughes (known in village as 'the Virgin Mary'!) and family. Children were Margaret, Jack and Robert.
Mrs Hughes and family (2 sons). Son Jack joined the Navy.
Mrs Naylor and family included Connie and one daughter. One son lost at sea during World War 1.
Mr & Mrs Worrall and family, a son, Sam, and daughter Clara. When old Mrs Worrall died, mother and daughter exchanged houses with Sam and family, who lived in Church Street at the time.
Mr & Mrs Adair and family. Mrs was second wife, Sam was son, and daughter Cissie died in 1918/19 flu epidemic. Daughter, Joyce, married a Garner. The family had a bulldog.
The Blackstock family at the Post office comprised of Mr Blackstock, son Jim and daughter Alice, who ran the Post Office until she got married.
Mr & Mrs Dickens and family, daughter May and son Harry. May worked for the tailor.
Mr. & Mrs. Renshaw (farmer).
Mr & Mrs Dickens and family. Hannah, Alice, Jack, Ted, Fred and Lizzie. Hannah married an Army deserter [Joe] who was hidden in the barn. When caught, he was shot.
Mr. & Mrs. Garner [daughter of Mr Adair] and family.
Mr. Jones [Police House], had a daughter who married the eldest son of John [Jack] Scott.
Mr. Moseley [farmer], had a large family, remembered as having shot himself in the foot by accident!
Rev. Smithett [vicarage] the Vicar was not very well liked in the village. He was succeeded by the Rev. Brassnet, who was well liked by Grandma Scott. He lived to be 100 years old.

123

Vicarage Lane

Hubbard family, children included Connie and Gilbert.

Charles, John and Lillian Drinkwater (farmers). They had a steam - powered thresher and a spark from the chimney set fire to a barn. The horse-drawn fire engine from Northwich attended and all the villagers helped to man the pumps to draw water from the brook.

Dickens family and 2 families of Hubbard

Left Hand side of High Street

Walter Scott and family.

Holden family, including Bridget, daughter.

Mrs Astles no known family.

Mr. & Mrs. Duncalf and family, including Dora, Fred, Ted, plus one other boy.

Miss Moss - The Old Hall. Later Dr. Love's son bought The Old Hall.

Mr. & Mrs. Southern, Mr Southern became Headmaster of School and moved to School Lane (next door to James and Mary Scott)

Mr. & Mrs. Holland, 2nd wife called May. Had a son by each wife.

Mrs. Cragg, widow and dressmaker was mother of Mrs Southern above.

Mrs. Holden. House later occupied by Walter Scott and family.

Mr. Priestner [retired farmer], adopted Alice Adair. He paid for the bells to be re-hung in Great Budworth Church

Doctor Love and Family

Mrs Bell - The George and Dragon

Church Street

Albert and Hannah Dickens
Mr & Mrs Simpson and family
Mr Birtles
Mr John Scott and family
Mr & Mrs Shingler
Mr & Mrs Hart
Mr & Mrs Cook
Mr Lever

Right Hand side of Church Street

Mr & Mrs Hubbard (corner Shop)
Mrs Drinkwater (farm)
Mr & Mrs Birtles and family
Mr & Mrs Worrall
Mr & Mrs Hughes and seven daughters
Mr Bowden
Mrs Thompson and later her daughter, Mrs Dolton (cottage at top of The Butts)

Anne Scott

Anne Scott - known as Nancy Scott - was born in Hawthorn Cottage, 62 High Street in 1922. Her parents were Walter and Mary. Walter died in 1963 when he was 77, but her mother lived until she was 100 and died in 1987. Walter himself was a remarkable character and it is a pity he never recorded his memories. He holds the record for service on Great Budworth Parish Council at 33 years from 1931 to 1964. Walter and Mary had a family of 10 children: 5 boys and 5 girls. In order of ages their names were Peter, Isobella (later Hocknull), Margaret (Peggy-later Haspell), Mary (later Holford), Walter, Malcolm, Alan, Anne, Vera (later Westwood) and John was the youngest. They lived at Hawthorn Cottage until about 1930 when they moved to Jasmine Cottage, No 54 High Street. This was the family home until 1981, by which time most of the brothers and sisters had moved to various parts of Cheshire and England. Anne lived in Great Budworth until 1953 when she went to New Zealand. She returned to England in 1959. Anne now lives in Antrobus and from the following account you will see that she has a remarkable memory for a lady 78 years young.

The Editors

Anne Scott aged 21

Great Budworth is regarded as one of the best known villages in Cheshire. The village church of St Mary and All Saints is one of the finest churches found in Cheshire. Until 1930 one of the customs observed in Great Budworth was a curfew rung in the evening at eight from April to October. The 'passing bell' was rung on the evening before a funeral. The bells were muffled and tolled for half an hour, ending with two strokes on each bell for a woman and three strokes for a man. For one hour before a funeral a muffled bell was tolled at intervals of three minutes. As the cortege came nearer the village, the interval between the strokes gradually decreased to half a minute, at which point the vicar would prepare to meet the cortege. I well remember first thing in the morning on the day of the funeral the residents of the village would draw all the curtains as a mark of respect. It was also a signal if anyone wanted to follow the cortege and go into church for the funeral service.

Isobella, my eldest sister, born during the 1st World War, remembers another old custom in the village: widows were allowed to bring their 'dough bread' to Bakery Cottage, courtesy of the owners, and use the oven to bake the bread. I guess there were many widows after the war.

Approaching the village via the Northwich - Warrington road, the A559 (the steep hill turning right off this road), at the top there is a right turn to The Mount, a little cul-de-sac of cottages on one side and gardens the size of allotments on the opposite side of some of them. At the bottom of the hill the pump house is situated where the pure spring water runs. One of Rowland Egerton Warburton's poems, "with ceaseless flow, springs from the earth below" is carved on a plaque above the pipe. I can remember clearly carrying water for drinking up the hill when I was old enough and strong enough. At one time the gates were locked late at night until next morning and the 'house' cleared up regularly - if I remember right - by the roadmen employed by the Runcorn Rural Council in whose area we were for many years.

The words on the plaque inside the porch at the George and Dragon were also penned by Rowland Egerton Warburton. He commissioned a number of distinguished Victorian architects to restore some of the houses on the right side of High Street, including the roofs and chimneys, with the use of locally made bricks. They were designed to be very tall with each one distinguishable as the patterns of bricks used in the chimneys are all different.

At the top of High Street and turning alongside the Churchyard wall to the right, there is a lane called South Bank - another cul-de-sac. At one end there is a lovely terrace of cottages and at the other end looking down below 'Hilly Bank' field there are splendid views of Marbury Mere and the Budworth end of the mere is, these days, owned by a Yachting Club.

On the other side of the Churchyard wall is School Lane, cobbled still, 17th century timber-framed cottages leading down to the village C of E school and a school house built originally as the Head Teacher's residence. When I was at the school, Mr Ernest Southern and his wife lived there. His mother lived next door to us, at 55 High Street.

The Scotts clockwise from back:
Peter, Peggy, Walter, Mary and Bella

School Lane leads to a very fine avenue of mature lime trees which leads to Westage Lane. Half way along it meets Farthings Lane, and a little further it leads to a footpath to Hield Farm. Farthings Lane got its name because it gave access to 4 allotments where the school field is now. Four farthings made a penny!! Opposite the exit of the Lime Avenue, on the other side of Westage Lane is the 'Sandhole' which was used by villagers to take their waste and rubbish.

Coming back to School Lane entrance, we turn right onto Church Street where there are also very ancient (some restored since 1945) cottages, originally with timber frames, and not two alike.

At the end of Church Street there is the bowling green and tennis court (the latter quite young). The bowling green and the Parish Hall opposite were originally all built on land donated to the village by the Egerton Warburtons of Arley Hall, after World War One. My father, being on the Parish Council, went to Arley Hall which was then owned by Mrs. Egerton Warburton, as her husband, Captain John Egerton Warburton, had been wounded and died of his wounds in 1915.

My father surveyed the land needed and so the village raised the money to develop and create the bowling green and the original building as storage and for members' meetings. Now, of course, it has been put to other uses and is the Village Hall.

This lane is named The Butts because in the days of archery in the medieval time of war, this is where they practised and learned their skills. At the bottom of the Butts the first field has always been used as pasture. Many years ago a pit was dug out in this field for clay to make bricks for cottages in the village. A kiln was built to bake the bricks. This field was called 'Brickkiln Field', in Cheshire dialect it became 'Brittlefield.'

Similarly the hill opposite Dene Hill leading to Comberbach was called 'Goodiers Brow' but became in Cheshire dialect 'Guddesbrow'

Up to the 19th Century the village had four public houses or inns: the 'George and Dragon' is the only one whose use was not changed. The other three were the 'White Hart' and the 'Saracen's Head', on the right side of High street and very close together. On the left side of Church Street was the 'Ring o' Bells'. These were all farm houses with adjacent land when I was born and now they are restored to residences.

Going back to my early days when our family was living at Hawthorn Cottage, we had regular visits in the village by all sorts of 'pedlars' coming to our door at the top of the hill and also the 'real' traditional gypsies who would camp out with their traditional caravans, drawn by a strong horse, on common land, usually in those days at Crow's Nest Lane off the Comberbach Road at Box Hedge. It was ideal for the gypsies here as the men could go into the woods at the Budworth end of Marbury park, and obtain the wood they needed to whittle and make clothes pegs. The women came into the village to sell these in large home-made baskets, along with elastic and little odds and ends and lucky charms. My mother always bought the pegs as she found them strong and well-made for the clothes to dry on the washing lines. I was always fascinated by their long, colourful dresses and large earrings and long strings of beads.

Often they had to bring children with them and sometimes the gypsy mother would ask for 'a crust' for the children and would usually get something better from my mother. Then there was the promise of good luck and blessings as she left us. A few days later we would see the caravans (no more than four) as they came up the hill, through the village to another suitable area to peddle their wares. The children went out to watch the dangling pots and pans and brightly-painted caravans passing through.

A pedlar my older sisters and I remember when we were growing up in Great Budworth was Mr. Sandbach who walked from Anderton. He came up the hill, always wearing a very long coat all the year round pushing his large deep box on wheels - it had long wooden shafts with which he pushed and sold all sorts of sewing tackle and yards of flannelette which I was told housewives made men's underwear and shirts with. He was quite a strange, quiet and polite man.

Another character who came regularly, was a man who also walked from Anderton. He had a sort of 'lisp' in his speech and before he knocked on the door he would call, *"Colty, Latey, Butty and Tud"* and he had a tray fitted with string hung round his neck. The translation is quite simple: Cottons, Laces (usually for shoes and boots), Buttons and Studs (for collars).

Then there was an Italian organ grinder with his monkey sitting on the top of the organ, which was wound up at the side. The monkey would do a few antics and we would be given a penny or two to take out to the street entertainment.

I've almost forgotten to mention the man who came on a bicycle with some sort of attachment to it and he made his presence known on the street by calling out asking if anyone had any scissors, knives and shears to sharpen. He worked the grinder with his foot on a pedal and I could not resist, like other children, going out to watch.

Another man came regularly with a small light weight horse and cart shouting *"Ragbones, Ragbones - any old rags."* He then waited on the street for people to come out with their rags, bones and rusty old pieces of metal which the villagers were unable to recycle themselves. My mother kept a ragbag hung up and she would ask me to go out and the ragman would empty it out on to his cart and he would give you back the empty bag and a 'donkey stone'- a square of soft stone that was used to clean the doorsteps. There were white/grey ones or if you were lucky deep cream coloured ones which my mother liked for her front door step at Jasmine Cottage.

My mother had a friend, Mrs Jackson who lived at Quebec Cottage at Budworth Heath, who used to draw a line round the edges of the step to finish it off - a great competition with the women - and sometimes she made a 'scribble' design all over or a 'red raddle' which when dry was a deep plum coloured design - a work of art.

Deliveries came to the village by farm horse and cart, and came up Dene hill once a week. There was Jim Hankey who lived with his parents at a little farm on the right at the crossroads at Wincham. He delivered vegetables and fruit - often grown locally by a farmer in the area, also imported fruit such as bananas, oranges, pomegranites, grapes and nuts at Christmas. He eventually married one of his customers, Nurse Goff, a Welsh lady, who lived in part of Rose Cottage, 57 High Street. This was rented by Arley Estates specifically for nurses and I remember three nurses from there all marrying local men.

While still living at Hawthorn Cottage, the milk came by a pony and trap each morning from Hield Farm at Aston-by-Budworth (top of Dark Lane Hill). The farmer was a Mr Platt and he had three daughters. The eldest measured the milk out into a tankard; in our case we had a quart-sized jug which my mother took out onto the street and which was filled by Miss Platt. However, if my mother required another quart this had to be collected at the farm when the milking session had finished. When we were old enough my younger sister, Vera, and I took over this task from our brothers. We came straight home from school at 4 o'clock to collect a quart-sized milk jug and walked up the avenue and over the stile leading to Hield Farm.

We always enjoyed it, even in winter time. I loved to see the farm animals and guinea fowl, which were quite rare in the area. The ploughman, Sam, was often back from the day's work in the fields with the two lovely shire horses, of which he was very proud and which he looked after well. We watched him take off all the trappings and then we could reach up and stroke their soft noses and they were so quiet and still when Sam was around. He would take the horses for a drink to a trough in the farmyard and in winter time stable them. Whilst waiting for the milk, we would watch another of the daughters in the dairy, putting the milk through the cooling and separating process, then thoroughly cleaning up the dairy and scalding out the tankards and measures. Everywhere looked so shiny and clean and I often compare it with the modern gadgets now that we have for washing and cleaning.

Sadly on one of these occasions, I think it was in 1935 and probably late summer time, my sister and I set off with the milk can after school and as we got nearer to the farm we saw smoke and disruption ahead on the farmyard and no cattle in sight. Once we got into the farmyard we were shocked to be told that the stock was being destroyed because it was infected with foot and mouth disease, which we had never heard of before. I don't remember whether we got milk, I doubt it, but it was the last visit we made to Hield Farm and one of the worst tragedies I remember in the area. It was such a disaster and shock to the Platt family as it was such a perfect model of a farm and the whole village was devastated.

I enjoyed my days at Great Budworth School and especially in spring and summer when we would be taken on nature walks in the area and could learn such a lot from the teacher. Sometimes we would be told to choose a specimen wild flower of our choice and when we had an art class to sketch and paint it. I could never get enough of that.

Now and then we would be allowed to walk to Arley Farm and Gardens, now much changed from those days. The owner then was the widow of Captain John Egerton Warburton and she had remarried. She decided to have a herd of Jersey cows and on one visit Mr Southern had got permission for the top class to visit the farm and we had a member of staff from Reaseheath Agricultural College, Miss Black, who demonstrated the preparation of the Jersey cow before milking and the whole process, then, of the product and hygiene, etc required. Then, we were allowed to walk in the garden and to go in the maze which was then at Arley Hall, but this had to be destroyed in war time as it needed too much attention and they were short of gardeners because of the war. It was fun and not easy to get out of the maze and these were happy memories in carefree days.

There were events which were started long before I was born and still continued until the Second World War. The 'Wakes' Social and Dance was a time for rejoicing - the Church's birthday as it is dedicated to St Mary and All Saints. All Saints' day had been changed in my days, to the first Sunday after November 8th. So during the following week there was a Dance and Parish Social. It was an old custom to eat Flummery as the old people called it. It was made from a mixture of boiled wheat, milk, sugar and spice of treacle. To please my father, my mother prepared a little for Wakes Sunday breakfast, but I never tasted it. My mother being Scottish, porridge was the right thing to eat for breakfast!

The usual preparations started long before the Wakes Social and it consisted of a Hot Pot Supper served first - the school rooms being the venue - and volunteers had to clear the two rooms which then had a screen which had to be pushed back and made into one room. The other half had a stage for the entertainers to perform on. Trestle tables and chairs were carried from outbuildings in the old vicarage yard, also crockery carried by the big girls in Miss Dean's class at Sunday School, and washed in the bowls ready for the supper. We all had a part to play in the organising of this event.

The Social was after the Hot Pot Supper and it was all solo songs for old village veterans and humorous poems by men who were wanting to entertain us and getting the whole audience to sing songs. School children of different ages sang in groups and recited poems which their teacher had taught them. The headmaster, Mr. Southern, always produced a stage play using the talent of the top class girls and boys still at school. The money raised was for the Church, the School, etc and was always a great success.

The annual fete was held at Belmont Park, courtesy of Colonel Moseley Leigh, normally at the end of July on a Saturday. It was a big event as a number of Comberbach families were part of the community, using the church and school in those days. This also raised funds for the School, the Church and the Local District Nursing Services. For some years the front part of Rose Cottage, High Street, was rented to the nurse by Arley Estate, so we had, for many years, a resident nurse in the village. There was a fete committee and here again the school chose a 'Queen of the Revels' (not a Rose Queen at Budworth fete). Mrs Southern would rehearse with the school children, out of hours, choose the costumes and train the Morris dancers, and they performed the Sailors' Hornpipe too. The traditional maypole dancers were trained by Miss Nancy Platt from Hield Farm. The procession was lined up on the School Field and the Barnton Silver Band was hired for the day. We walked down High Street, which was decorated across the street from bedroom window to bedroom window opposite, with flags and bunting. Everyone put out a Union Jack. We proceeded to the bottom of the hill turning right to the Cock Inn and on to Belmont Park Lodge gates. The village policeman, wheeling his bicycle, headed the procession and the Morris dancers, 12 of them plus the leader, partly danced and marched to the tune, usually 'Bonnie Dundee' with the Band behind us. Having led the Morris dancers for two years consecutively, I have a very vivid recollection of that.

The usual throne for the Queen and her Court was prominent and nicely decorated by Mrs Southern who was very artistic in many ways. There were marquees and a big area for the onlookers was prepared. There were handicrafts for sale, donated food to buy and lots of the usual stalls with hoopla, skittles, coconut shies and the weight of a pig to guess and receive as a prize. The marquees were for refreshments and portable toilets were provided. The Winnington Boy Scouts always were allowed to have a camp on part of the Belmont Estate and always did their good deed by helping to clean up the mass of rubbish, etc over such a large area. Afterwards there was always a dance on the lawn in front of the hall, usually grown-up couples paid a bit extra for their admission ticket to dance. I looked forward to being able to do that but the war came and fetes ceased to be part of village life. I do not recall having rain on the day of the fete, ever.

Rose Fete 1939

Before the Second World War there were quite a few 'cottage industries' in Great Budworth. For example

Mr Harry Holland at 56 High Street, sold milk, eggs and potatoes. He was also a cobbler and looked after the Vicarage garden.

Mr Harry Walton and Son were tailors and employed a man and woman who cycled from Wincham. They also employed 2 or 3 part-time women or apprentices.

Mr Matty Moores who lived at 17 High Street was a builder and his wife was a dressmaker and tailoress.

Mr Peter Adair at 15 High Street ran the village bakery.

Mr Sam Worrall at 14 High Street, or Mere View as it was called then, was a joiner and undertaker.

Mr Fred Adair at 10 High Street was a painter and decorator.

Mr Walter Hughes at 11 High Street repaired bicycles and motor cars.

Mrs Hart and daughter Mrs Carter at Providence Cottage, Church Street made lunches and teas for cycling clubs, and catered for parties and funerals.

My father Walter Scott was a draughtsman at ICI but he had two hobbies which he used for the benefit of the village. He was a keen photographer and had his own dark room. He took photographs of weddings and fetes, etc. Also he repaired 'wireless' sets and repaired electrical faults.

Mr Renshaw from Saracen's Head was an agent for the Friendly Society of Foresters. They distributed clothing, fabrics, food etc. This ceased during the War.

Delivering milk in High Street, Great Budworth

When Winston Churchill announced over the wireless in September 1939 that we had declared war with Germany, we were a large family living in Great Budworth village - although some of the older members of our family had already flown the nest. I do remember that there had been premonitions that this was inevitable as there was a lot of talk about air raid shelters, and ARP civilian volunteers being recruited in the major cities. Little did we know how our lives and life style would change for six long years.

I was 17 years old that year and had, in July 1939, just completed my education. Earlier in the year a Red Cross Society First Aid Course was offered in Knutsford Division of the Red Cross Society, to be held weekly in Arley Hall. I joined and in October 1939 the course was completed, examinations were conducted, written and practical and I gained my certificate. We had a relative who was the matron in a children's hospital in Liverpool and, during her frequent visits to us, she always did her best to try to persuade me to go for a career in nursing. Eventually I succumbed but had to wait two or three months before I could apply to the hospital of her choice - one had to be seventeen and a half years old then. I spent the time over that period gaining some experience in what was known as the White Cross Hospital or Annexe of Warrington General Hospital where most of the patients were old and terminally ill. This was more than enough to qualify me for the Red Cross Home Nursing certificate. Early in 1940, I was accepted as a probationer nurse in a large training hospital in Smithdown Road, Liverpool. I began in the men's Orthopaedic ward.

By this time, two of my brothers had been called up and both were serving overseas in the army. Britain was very much on the defensive and the bomb raids increased. One by one the Germans were invading European countries and occupying them, they were very dark days. Marbury Hall and the grounds were taken over to be used as an army camp and troops marching along all the country roads became a very common sight. I was on duty in the ward when news came through that the evacuation of our armed forces, which had been on the retreat for some weeks on the Continent, had started to take place and it was then all we could think about as everyone had someone involved whom they were concerned and anxious about. We knew that one of my brothers had been in France since the beginning and the other was in Athens, Greece by that time. The next morning when I went on duty I could see that during the night some of the patients had been moved in order to make space for emergency cases. I soon discovered that we had two men, weather-beaten and unshaven, sleeping soundly and I knew at once that they must be casualties of the Dunkirk evacuation. Our usual patients were keeping quiet and whispering amongst themselves not wishing to disturb them. The sister on the ward explained that they were two Norwegian seamen who had joined in the rescue and evacuation of their allies - not injured but needing a few days' care and rest after their ordeal. Later in the day they 'came round' and, although they could hardly speak a word of English, expressed their gratitude and thanks by their expressions and smiles of joy when they found themselves safe and warm - no words were needed!

We eventually heard, first from the Red Cross and then the War Office, that my brother serving in France had survived the Dunkirk evacuation, suffered a shoulder wound and was in hospital 'somewhere in England'. When he recovered he was granted a few days' leave at home before rejoining his unit in the Grenadier Guards. We learned that he was in the sea waiting to get on a rescue vessel when he was hit by a bullet - the enemy were strafing them in the water - pulled out of the water and that particular group were put ashore on the Welsh coast. Here they were warmly greeted and taken care of by housewives standing by to help in any way, providing hot drinks, etc as well as medical care, dry clothing and comfort.

After four months' nurse training in Liverpool, I had reached the stage where a probationer had to make up her mind whether she would continue her nursing career and complete the three-year training period, commence attending lectures and sitting yearly exams. Individual interviews with the matron were arranged and, for some reason or other, at that time I had decided, if I could conjure up the courage, to say I did not wish to continue. So, much to the dismay of the matron, the sister of the ward I had been working in and also my relative, I left and returned home to Great Budworth.

I applied to ICI for employment in the offices and in January 1941, I commenced at Winnington, cycling to and fro from Great Budworth.

For as long as I can remember Providence Cottage, Church Street, Great Budworth, owned by Mrs Hart and her daughter and son-in-law, had a very popular business, using one of the very spacious rooms as a tea room, serving home-made food and home-grown local produce, regularly used by Cycling Clubs as their meeting place and for refreshments. Villagers and visitors to the area also patronised it.

The Cyclists' Caterer

I was a friend of the grandaughter, who also worked at ICI and when the first troops at Marbury discovered this tea room, business became very brisk and the favourite item on the menu became fresh poached egg on toast, with tea and buttered home-made scones and jam, with the added bonus of two sprightly country lasses serving them. My friend's mother was a very good pianist and we often had a sing-song round the piano so the customers got light entertainment too and joined in. We knew they would soon be in the thick of it. During the first two years of the war, they did apply to the Ministry of Food, for catering allowances of food, being well-established, but later they had to close as it was impossible to keep up the standards.

During 1941, I believe we civilians were getting used to regulations; carrying identity cards, gas masks and ration books, also clothing coupons and queues. Ladies' handbags were now available, made in leather still, moulded to the shape of the gas mask, with zipped pockets on the outside for cash and identity card, and much more attractive than the free issue cardboard box and such like. If not already innovative and practical one had to try to become so-minded and make certain sacrifices to help the war effort. Slogans began to appear on notice boards everywhere *'Dig for Victory'*, *'Make do and Mend'*, *'Make something new out of something old'* (this applied not only to clothing but to utensils and furniture, etc) and, with regard to National Security and enemy spies amongst us, *'Careless talk costs lives'*.

Still living at home with our parents were one sister, Vera, and one brother, John - who would not be able to serve in the armed forces because he had become a victim of poliomyelitis when he was four years old - and myself. We all agreed to give up sugar in all our beverages in order that our mother could continue making preserves using our home produce. We had a very large garden with a variety of fruit trees, soft fruit bushes, and grew a few rows of early potatoes and vegetables and herbs. At the far end of the garden we had a penned area with about two dozen poultry supplying us with eggs enough before the war. We therefore decided to give up all our egg rations and be entitled to the equivalent amount of imported feed. We had always used potato peelings, vegetable trimmings, together with 'chats', available free from farmers in the area, left in the fields after potato harvesting was completed.

We had a large dry cellar, transformed as a store room, and we were very glad of this when war time came. In the good-laying period we were able to preserve supplies surplus to our requirements in a special egg preserver and isinglass. With some reluctance, and the deed was not performed by any of us, we would kill one of the non-laying flock and we also kept Aylesbury ducks too, to help the food supply and keep the grass down among the fruit bushes. It was quite a lot of work and we all had to help. I for one hated the 'cleaning out of the houses' sessions, but enjoyed the gardening very much.

In the meantime on the battle front the Germans, ever on the offensive, were pushing our armies towards eastern Europe and finally invaded Greece and another evacuation of our men took place. As another brother, along with the liaison officer he was serving with in Athens, were caught up in all this and after a long silence with no word of him, we eventually received a War Office telegram, towards the end of 1941, to say that he was 'missing and believed killed'.

It was going to be a long and difficult year ahead before we received any more news of him.

We were still waiting and hoping when a third brother, not living at home and in a civilian job - also a 'reserve soldier' having been trained in the Scots Guards - was called up and posted down south where there were huge concentrations of forces in readiness for the threat of war in North African territories and for defending Britain from invasion. The pounding of London continued and we knew at first hand about all the tragedies in and around London and the south coast as our eldest brother had been living in London for many years and was in the front line as a member of the Metropolitan Police force. We also had at least two families of close relatives living in the northern suburbs of London. One evening, an aunt, uncle and their teenage daughter arrived unexpectedly on our doorstep carrying only the essentials. They had driven by car from Dagenham, Essex where they had lived for some years and had put up with nights in shelters, sleepless nights and could bear it no longer. They were nervous wrecks and, when a bomb proved to be a direct hit on the detached house next door and their roof was damaged, they just fled and luckily their car remained undamaged. They stayed with us and in time settled in Cheshire from then on.

It was not long before our spare living space was filled again as following a survey of available billets in the area, my parents were approached and asked to billet two servicemen. They agreed and the two duly arrived fully equipped, including two M.O.Defence 'labelled' bicycles, serving in the RAF - one a Scotsman and the other from Lincolnshire - Jock and Marshall they became known to us. Their mission and the location where they performed it, were 'secret' so the 'Careless talk costs lives' was applied. We asked no questions, made them very much at home and we all got on well. Once they had established whatever it was they were establishing it had to be manned day and night, and guarded. They took it in turns to be on duty all night or all day, with a change about arranged between themselves, and a seven-day week. Jock made himself very useful in return for the many extras my mother provided - such as doing their laundry, which they were supposed to do themselves. Jock regularly cleaned all the silver and brasses and Marshall would do some gardening - they were both married men!

We had realised that their work was something to do with assisting the anti-aircraft gun emplacements in the area, manned by the army and the searchlight units also in the area. Enemy aircraft were managing to get through the coastal barrage and ICI and the industrial town of Northwich were well-known targets inland, so the decoy proved to be very effective later that year.

I don't remember how long Jock and Marshall were with us or when the two-man team was changed. Next came two Georges, both from Glasgow, younger and single. When they had 'sussed out' the entertainment in the area they cycled, when one or other was off duty, and discovered Winnington Recreation Club where wartime dances were held. Having met them, it was not long before some of the girls I worked with discovered where their base was and they admitted they were all 'green with envy'. This was especially so when they learned much later that my remaining sister at home had volunteered for the WRNS, and as a hairdresser who would otherwise have been drafted into industry or other women's services, she had decided on this option. Once my sister left, one of the Georges, who happened to be a very good hairdresser by trade, was only too pleased to provide this service, free, and as I recall that was my only war-time 'perk'.

The airmen were still billeted with us and, towards the end of February, I was at work when one of the departmental heads came into the office and approached me quietly, delivering a message which had been received over the 'phone from my father who was based at ICI, Lostock. It was to say how sorry he was to tell me that one of my brothers had been killed on active service and my father had requested that I may be allowed to go home as my mother was in shock. I did not know at that point which of the three brothers it was. I soon learned on arriving home that it was Walter, our second eldest brother in the Scots Guards, who had been killed. The next few weeks were very difficult but one had to carry on the fight. During this period my sister left, having been accepted in the WRNS.

Another sister living in the area, whose husband had been called up and was serving in the RAF, had no ties and applied for a NAAFI job in the area along with another woman. Both had to be able to drive a large truck, converted by the army as a mobile shop-cum-hot drinks service, serving the searchlight and the anti-aircraft gun sites, on the spot. They were on duty various hours and, with the blackout restrictions and the locations of these sites being rural, it was no easy job but they were so welcomed and relied upon - for cigarettes, etc - and they would also post letters for the men. They were provided with a uniform, shoes, etc, similar to the ATS, and had to be able to do

141

the basics such as changing a wheel.

Towards the end of the year, and about twelve months after we received that telegram concerning my brother's last movements before the evacuation of Greece-fleeing armies, we received a letter from a soldier in a German POW hospital, written on behalf of my missing brother who was in the next bed to him in that same hospital, but too weak to write himself. It was a great relief and, because all POW letters were censored, we did not know where the hospital was, but we gathered that our brother had been very ill and was now slowly recovering. Soon afterwards we received official news from the Red Cross and War Office just to say he was alive and in a POW camp. The Red Cross then contacted us, providing us with a lot of support and we were allowed to send letters, through them, according to the Geneva convention, so once more we had contact and could at least write to him on special forms provided. These were all censored at our end - words could sometimes be obliterated or in some cases letters destroyed. We now had another incentive and a strong commitment to raising funds for the Red Cross Society.

Once our brother was traced to be in a POW hospital, through the Red Cross, we were allowed to send what they called 'Invalid Comforts Parcels' on a regular basis. To obtain these 'invalid comforts', especially in the case of special items of food difficult to buy in war time, we gave our coupons in ration books and in particular all our sweets coupons from our ration books. The whole page was cut out of our books (4 of them in total) and deposited at the local shop, so that the shopkeeper could order from the wholesaler he or she patronised. The only items allowed in an invalid comforts parcel were sticks of pure barley sugar and a one pound weight, solid block, of plain chocolate per parcel sent. Some cigarettes were allowed and were welcomed by the POWs because they could trade them for other items they needed through the German guards at the camp who were glad to get the cigarettes in exchange. My brother had eventually been discharged from the hospital and moved to a POW camp high in the mountains on the borders of Austria and Yugoslavia, known as STALAG 383. This camp was for NCOs only and, according to the Geneva convention, they could be refused to be sent to work by the Germans. Here, Red Cross parcels could still be sent to the men - one every three months - the list of items allowed had to be strictly adhered to and the packing details also. Items included some types of canned food, toiletries, shaving brush but not razor blades and, in between each three months we were knitting khaki-coloured, woollen helmets and pullovers and socks or stockings. The prisoners were housed in wooden huts accommodating about eight men and, of course, they had no heating in very cold conditions in the winters. Following all the Red Cross instructions, the parcel, when ready for posting to a Red Cross centre in the UK, had to be of certain dimensions - perfectly square - and for this we used a tin box. It was wrapped in brown paper with string, then wrapped in hessian or, as we sometimes acquired one, an empty strong cotton flour bag and the whole thing was sewn up with strong linen thread. When completed with a calico label, which we had to address with Indian ink to be waterproof, we had to check the exact weight allowed and to achieve this we weighed every single thing - the paper, the string, the hessian and every item before we packed it, after our first experience.

This may seem pedantic but these were the regulations and from the Red Cross's point of view, when transporting, loading, unloading and storing before distribution, these parcels of uniform size and weight meant not an inch of space was wasted, plus the fact that it had a 100% chance of arriving intact - certainly my brother received all his in good condition. At this point, I will say that, when our brother was repatriated, it was very interesting to hear, and see, some of the photographs, postcard size and somehow produced and developed (in sepia colour) in secret in camp, proof of the fact that all the packing materials - string, tins and canvas - was never wasted in that particular camp. There were Kiwi, Aussie and British POWs from every walk of life and, rarely given exercise out of camp, they organised themselves according to their various skills and kept themselves busy and occupied, also providing their own entertainment by putting on shows and making costumes from all the bits and pieces from the parcel wrappings. The photographs included groups outside the hut and a photo of the annually elected 'Miss Stalag 19..', according to year of office. 'She' was always dressed in a very long, well-designed gown with the usual sash over one shoulder and tied in a bow at the waist on the other side, with the title "MISS STALAG 19.." printed on the sash. The outfit would not stay intact for the whole year I am sure, but it looked good. I understand that the popular choice was usually a tall, blonde Australian!

Once we were registered with the Red Cross as supporters and willing fund-raisers, we were asked to participate in a scheme they named The Red Cross Agricultural Penny a Week Fund. This scheme was introduced to cover weekly collection in rural areaswhere it was not practical to have a street collection. We agreed to do this and the Red Cross provided all the publicity and collecting boxes, posters and so on. First of all we had to knock on all doors and ask families to pledge one penny a week. I do not recall anyone refusing to contribute and in many cases more than one penny was contributed. We were designated quite a large area to cover and so I did the outlying, scattered homes and farms, at the weekend, cycling around with my box. Our mother managed the village during the week. We raised funds in lots of other ways by organising a dance occasionally in the winter months and selling any produce from the garden which we could not use to people we knew and, when we delivered it, they put anything they wished in our box.

The youngest member of the family, our disabled brother, having finished school, and being eligible for a wartime Government scheme for disabled males to go for various training, applied and was accepted, although it meant he would have to live away from home for the training he required. He chose to do a practical and theoretical engineering course, so had to live in 'digs' in Birmingham and later when he decided to specialise in structural engineering, a period in Lincolnshire and, by the end of the war, he was home and qualified as a structural engineering draughtsman for ICI.

Mary Scott with Vera, Anne and John sitting on the cushion

All the above events left me the only member of the family at home and, inevitably, I very much wanted to join in the women's services. One day when I was in Chester shopping I passed the WAAF recruitment offices and, on the spur of the moment, I went in and asked for an application form, filled it in, there and then, said nothing about it to anyone and subsequently was called to Chester for an interview and medical. It was not long before I received a letter from Chester explaining that I had been accepted but, when they had applied for my release from ICI Winnington, they had refused to release me. I was very disappointed and angry about it at the time but there was nothing I could do about it.

By the end of 1943 the bombing raids by the German Luftwaffe over the UK were on the decrease - the Battle of Britain in that sense was won with all the support and commitment of the Brits and all our allies. My brother living in London and his wife felt it was safe enough for those of our family who were able to at the time, to spend Christmas 1943 with them and other relatives and friends in London. This visit to London persuaded me in the following spring to go on frequent weekend visits, via train from Hartford, when cheap, main line railway excursions were introduced - leaving Friday evening and returning late Sunday night. I did not at first venture from where I was staying in the north-west suburbs to the West End on shopping sprees as I was advised not to do this, as was my sister-in-law, unless my brother was off-duty to accompany us. After dark, if the siren wailed, we took shelter under the staircase cupboard as, at that stage in the war, it meant a very early warning that the old enemy 'planes had sneaked very close to the coast line. With all the sophisticated defence weapons we had by then, coupled with the very effective barrage balloons, it meant that it was not necessary to go outside and run for shelters or the underground station nearby because the enemy aircraft would never reach its target and in a short time the 'all clear' siren would have wailed.

On one of these visits south, in spring 1944, I was invited to spend a two-week holiday with my aunt and uncle who lived in Horley, Surrey, close to Gatwick Airport. Gatwick was taken over at the outbreak of the war, as many other airports were, as an operational base for the RAF and Fleet Air Arm usage - heavily guarded, etc. Gatwick was, at the time of my visit, a base for bombing operations over Germany and their crews, workshops, repair shops and all amenities and changes had been made.

Local people, mostly women, were also employed. My uncle was the General Manager there in charge of the civilian staff - he was a pilot in the Royal Flying Corps, which became the nucleus of the RAF. Since 1918, he had been employed in major aircraft industries, specialising in aircraft design and, at the outbreak of war in 1939, he was transferred to the Air Ministry in London, the preparation for serving at Gatwick. I had visited them for holidays before the war and was well aware of my uncle's enthusiasm for aviation, and their only son, our cousin, was serving in the RAF bombing squadrons but not based at Gatwick at the time. So, I was not at all surprised when on the second day of my visit my uncle said that all arrangements had been made (security check on me, etc) for me to be shown around the whole operation. This was one of the highlights of my wartime experiences, quite unique, and I relished it.

I was taken to a hanger where a Wellington bomber was receiving minor repairs before continuing operational service. One of the RAF engineers in the hangar asked if I would like to sit in the pilot's seat and I, of course, said, "Yes please" and I climbed up. It was quite a height and I sat there for a few minutes. I next saw Wellington bombers being loaded and prepared for the next operation - usually night operations, returning at dawn.

I was taken around hangars refitted as workshops where civilian workers were folding parachutes into a satchel type of container, with all the cords and attachments, in a special way for which they had been trained and supervised by a WAAF in uniform. Every precaution was taken so that when the pilot or his crew put one on, in an emergency it would never fail them. There were other civilian workers at the other side of the hangar, which was fitted with benches also, who were carefully examining parachutes which had been used to make a landing and retrieved and before being put to use again, checked to make sure there were no flaws or holes in the chute itself and/or the cords or leather harness support. Again a senior, civilian lady at the end of the line inspected each one and either rejected or passed the parachute.

I then had a meal in the canteen with them all and felt very privileged and very proud of my countrymen and women for the part they were playing. Teamwork and dedication was so important for our offensive and ultimate victory.

I made another visit to London at August Bank holiday weekend 1944, with my eldest sister, who at the time was living in Great Budworth, and was employed by ICI Winnington as one of the eight chauffeuses at the Garage. They were on shift work (two on each shift) always on call throughout the day and night - replacing the men who usually did this job and had been called up for active service. This visit proved to be another highlight of my experiences. With the threat of air raids now unlikely in daylight, despite devastation everywhere, there was such an air of confidence on the faces of the people now crowding the streets. Many allied servicemen, in uniform and easily identified, were getting leave from bases in the UK and Europe and were making straight for London where more entertainment, often provided by their various HQs in London and serving men themselves, was available.

One evening my sister and I attended a dance held in the suburb where we were staying with relatives, and met two Canadians - one serving in the army and the other in the air force. They asked us to meet up with them in the city centre the next day and show them the 'remaining' sights - a lot of overseas men were being ripped off by the 'wise boys' at that time, so we promised to protect them from these 'rackets' and advise them where to go to buy their gifts to take back home. They had acquired complimentary tickets for the four of us to attend a baseball match the next day, at Wembley Stadium, between Canadian and American teams then on leave and we looked forward to this. It proved to be a very exciting day, with good weather and long queues to stand in as ticket holders and non-ticket holders went through the same turnstiles - and it was such a great event - there had been nothing like it since the war started. Our companions said that we must shout and cheer for the Canadian team only. The guest of honour duly arrived, escorted by 'top brass' American and Canadian officers and we were suddenly aware that 'she' was the then, Mrs Winston Churchill. After the two teams lined up below us had been introduced and inspected by the VIPs they were shown to their seats and we were quite astonished to find that we were a little to the right of the group, in the row behind and so had a good view of Mrs Churchill as she stood in her seat and presented the trophy to the winning American team, congratulating them and commiserating, no doubt, with the Canadian team. There was no opportunity in those days to record things with one's camera as films were not obtainable and there was a clear absence of cameras representing the press - these events were not advertised - and after all we were still fighting on other fronts.

Many visits to London followed and in early 1945 it was great to see how the people were clearing up the unsightly rubble although it left great gaps here and there reminding us of what had been there before. Once again the shops were selling a wider range of goods in big departmental stores and some accessories, not on coupons, were being made to brighten up an outfit. My brother's wife was employed in one of the large stores in Knightsbridge where, before the war they had a roof-top garden where refreshments were served. The store was reopened that year and, as it has not been damaged, was restored almost to its former glory, complete with a stream where wild ducks lived and little fountains played - quite an oasis. We always had refreshments up there and looking out over the city of London, free once more, was exhilarating. Unfortunately, it is not there now and skyscrapers and taller buildings along with pollution, I suppose, would not be environmentally friendly.

Although we all realised that this day was getting nearer, I seem to recall that, despite the fact that what was going on in Europe was well reported, we did not know that the Germans were on the point of surrendering - the final, quite sudden announcement over the radio by Winston Churchill in London was quite a shock and an anti-climax, but a pleasant one for a change.

The celebrations and arrangements for same immediately began all over the country and we did our share of this in Great Budworth. However, quite a large number of families all over the country were waiting for the return of their serving men, from overseas particularly, and some of these were still fighting the enemy in the Far East. We as a family celebrated in great style at Christmas 1945/New Year 1946, when we unsealed a barrel of home-made blackberry wine, specially kept for this occasion and very potent it turned out to be. We made a quantity of home-made wines during the war using a variety of fruits from the garden. There was damson wine, raspberry syrup for colds, rhubarb wine and cider made from very small often windblown apples and plenty of blackberries there for the picking in autumn.

I am sure that all those who are old enough to remember and were involved in the last war, at a time like this remember their families, friends and neighbours, perhaps, who lost their lives as a consequence. We as a family lost our brother in February 1942, only 26 years of age; our cousin in the RAF from Horley, who was sadly and ironically killed on return from a bombing raid over Kiel Canal, Germany, crashing just over the coast of Britain with all crew killed, just three weeks before VE day. He was aged 21 years and an only child.

Also, someone we got to know very well, Captain John Dean, the padre for the Royal Norfolk regiment which was based at Marbury camp for quite a long spell in 1941 before eventually they were 'kitted out' with tropical kit which suggested the Far East as their destination. Once the men realised that they would not be getting leave to visit their families in the southern-east counties, before leaving the UK, they called on surrounding villages of Marbury to ask for temporary accommodation for their wives, if married. The Royal Norfolk regiment had a very good reputation with residents in the towns and villages around Marbury and their padre had called on us and asked my parents to accommodate his wife, which we gladly did. For six weeks approximately they stayed with us and they were a delightful couple, with two daughters at home, growing up. In October 1941, overnight, the camp was evacuated to another base up north and shipped overseas to arrive in Singapore in February 1942, when it had already fallen to the Japs and they were all taken prisoner immediately.

No doubt most people have heard of what they suffered in those horrific camps until August 1945, when eventually those who had survived were brought home. Sadly, John Dean was not one of these and we learned this later when his wife visited us from their home in Norfolk. She came to tell us and to thank my parents for those few weeks they stayed with us - she wanted to visit the area again and the place where she had said 'goodbye' to her husband. We appreciated this and felt very grateful and we also thought she was very brave indeed to do this.

All these memories of village life are treasured and, together with my Second World War memories, I have relived both good and bad experiences. I am pleased that the village retains the charm and welcoming atmosphere it had years ago.

Anne Scott

Kathleen Harris

Kathleen Harris never lived in Great Budworth. From 1930 she was married to Sam Harris who was an agent to the Arley Estate and as such they were good friends to Great Budworth. Kathleen lived at Arley, Appleton and now lives in Harrogate. She was a founder member and stalwart of Great Budworth Women's Institute which has and does play an important part in village life. She was president of the Women's Institute for many years and served at County Federation level. Kathleen celebrated her 90th birthday on the 15th August 2000.

The Editors

Kathleen Harris

There has been some discussion in the newspapers recently about the suitability of certain football players to represent Scotland and Wales and as I was not born in Great Budworth I can only hope that fifty years of close association with the village will allow me to 'play for Budworth' as it were.

My name is Kathleen Harris and my marriage in 1930 to the Agent for the Trustees for the Arley Estate brought me immediately into the life of the village. We were at Arley for almost 20 years and then moved to Appleton, not much further away and most of which once belonged to Arley.

When in 1932 a branch of the Women's Institute was started by Miss Elizabeth Egerton-Warburton, a new world opened up and members took every opportunity of using the expert tuition which was available through the County Federation. We sewed, we sang, we danced, we cooked, we painted and also the aim was to reach the highest possible standard. As the 'anxious Thirties' ended in the declaration of war in 1939, for the next six years our chief object in life was to make what seemed to us starvation rations last to the end of the week. We all had our ways of stretching the rations - enlarging the meagre butter ration by adding milk drop by drop, concocting recipes like 'fatless' cake, making oatmeal biscuits and who can forget the dried milk, the Spam, the tinned sausages, and when the Government allowed us to have unrationed meat pies once a week (to compensate for the British Restaurants available in towns) the humble pie became a gourmet dish.

Poster appealing for Rose Hips, 1942

In high summer the Old Hall became a jam factory. Realising that all the fruit in country gardens was falling off the branches because no-one had any sugar to make it to jam the Government, through the WIs instituted a scheme by which fruit was brought into a centre. Helpers stirred large brass jam pans day after day (mainly blackcurrants and raspberries) but of course it was strictly controlled - countless pounds of unrationed sugar could not be put in the hands of sugar hungry women, so a domestic science officer was in charge of an area to ensure that the right amount of sugar was allocated for the weight of fruit brought and that the end result was what it should be in quantity and quality. The jam-makers were considered rewarded by being allowed to spread the froth from skimming impurities from the boiling pans on their bread at tea time. The gleaming jars went off to the shops in town. And so six years of anxiety and restrictions are compressed into a page of foolscap; it was well into the fifties when rations were gradually increased and life returned to normal (if it ever did!).

The Womens Institute.

The WI Badge

In 1951 the County Federation proposed a competition for a Village Scrap Book, though the entries turned out to be quite serious village histories. For Great Budworth's volume we were very fortunate to have drawings by Mr Fletcher, who then ran a school at Belmont, and hand-scripted text by Miss Love. Known sources and local knowledge resulted in our being highly commended by the judges and ours was one of a selection on show at the Annual meeting of the Standing Conference on Local History in London.

A SCRAP BOOK
OF THE DISTRICT OF
GREAT BUDWORTH
COMPILED BY MEMBERS
OF THE
WOMENS INSTITUTE
IN THE YEAR OF THE
FESTIVAL OF BRITAIN
1951

The WI Scrap Book 1951

Our next effort was to record the age of hedges in the parish. A passing stranger might be puzzled to see a group of three or four women closely inspecting a length of hedge in summer (too late for bird nesting and too early for blackberrying) and why, occasionally, did one of them take a number of long strides and then rejoin the others and continue to peer into the hedge? This was the accepted method of dating a hedge: a thirty-yard stretch was marked out and then the number of different plants recorded and multiplied by ten, and that is the approximate age of the hedge. Naturally as fields have been divided most hedges are mainly hawthorns and only a hundred or two years old but we did have some 'prizes.' We knew the monks of Norton Priory were reputed to fish in the Mere and sure enough one side of the lane had a five hundred-year-old count.

For hundreds of years men and women of Great Budworth have worked at Arley and the shortest way, on foot, was by the footpath starting at the end of the lane by Hill Top farm, and sure enough there was another ancient one. When we were closing our list of six, five, four and three hundred-year-old stretches of hedge, Mrs Littler on the Mount found the hedge at the bottom of her garden was amongst the oldest so far discovered.

Then we turned to houses and listed the houses that had evidently once been thatched and found an impressive number, though in the watercolour painting by Mr Piers Egerton-Warburton in 1880 those at the bottom half of High Street had been tiled.

How else could we extend our knowledge of the village? The next proposal was to have a complete list of field names. This was available in the tithe maps at the County Record Office in Chester but the Estate map used by Mr Scott for the 'scrap' book did not record the names of fields in the whole parish as some belonged to Belmont or private owners. However, by filling in the gaps from the tithe maps in Chester a fairly comprehensive list was obtained and a reduced copy for easier handling was made by Mrs. Wilkinson.

These surveys were carried out by WI members and, as I continued my membership after I went to live in Appleton, and as I felt that exploring these facts which form the bones of the parish was most interesting, I spent a good deal of time on the old Roman Road which must appear from time to time on the Stretton to Budworth road. (I was told that years ago it was a custom after Evening Service to go for a walk along the 'cosy', the straight road in front of Belmont.) Could this charming name be an adaptation of 'causeway' which is often associated with Roman roads?

The most regularly occurring event both at Budworth and Arley, both of which involved me, was the Whist drive. The amounts of money raised were small and I prefer to think of a Whist Drive as an integral part of village social life. Children were probably born with the gene, heard the words constantly as they grew up and at the appropriate age joined their parents at the green baize tables.

Arranging one followed an established pattern. A meeting was called and diaries were produced to check the date of the full moon. Why? Country roads are exceedingly dark, there are no street lights and everyone travels on foot or by bicycle. Our catchment area was wide - Antrobus, Comberbach, Marston, Wincham and of course Arley. Having chosen the nearest Friday to the full moon (Friday because the school room hadn't to be cleaned for the next morning) we could soon settle the other time-honoured details.

Some four hundred years ago, William Shakespeare was writing 'A Midsummer Night's Dream' and a gathering of villagers met to celebrate the marriage of Theseus and Hippolyta.

'Doth the moon shine the night we play our play?
A Calendar, a calendar, look in the almanack;
Find out moonshine, find out moonshine.'

I do not suppose the reason for the question was the same as ours, but it makes a very apt quotation to illustrate the meetings which were held throughout the country for who knows how long, and reminds me in my old age of all those years of 'finding out moonshine'.

Budworth Mere

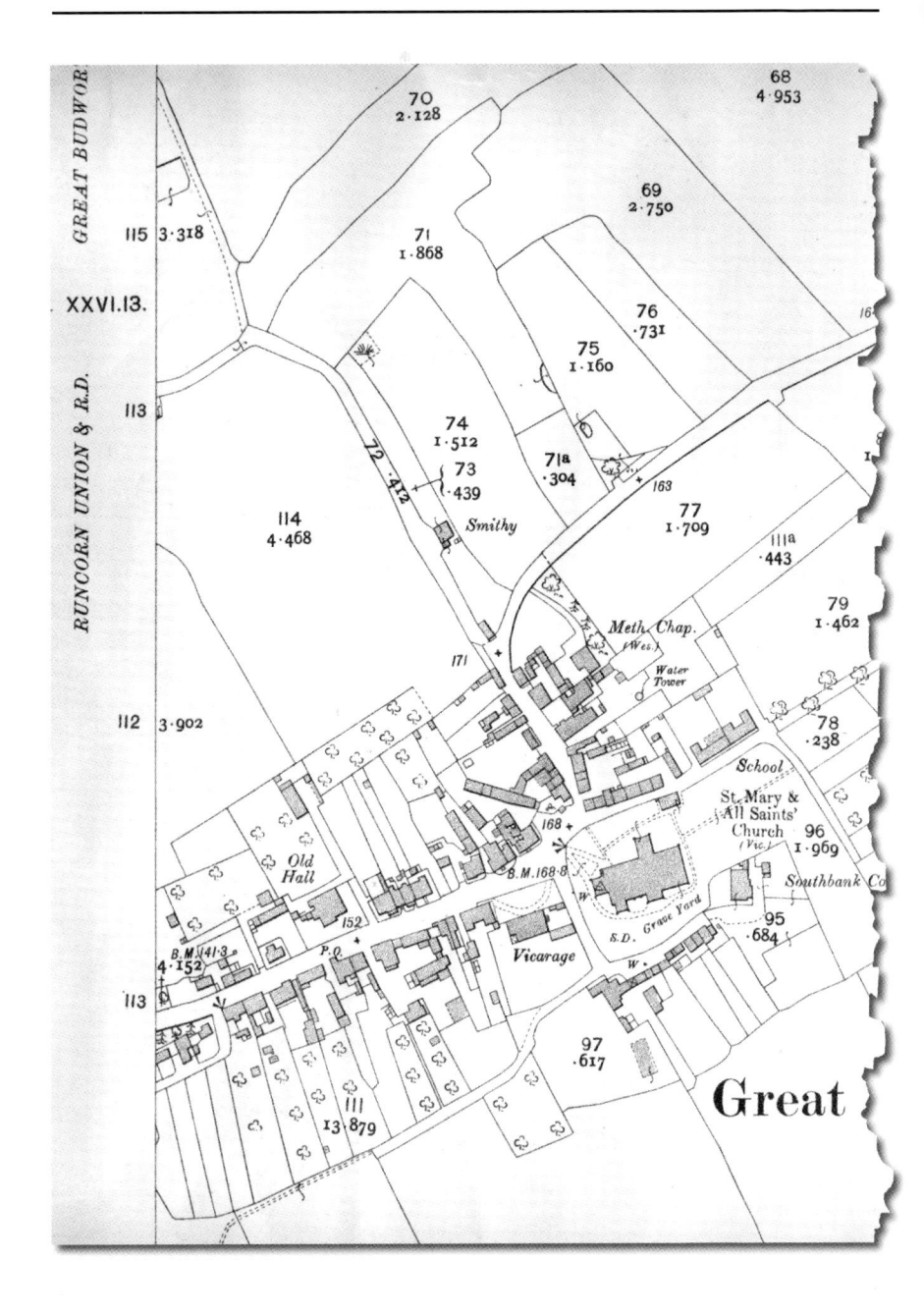

The Village of Great Budworth: 1910 Series Ordnance Survey Map

Budworth

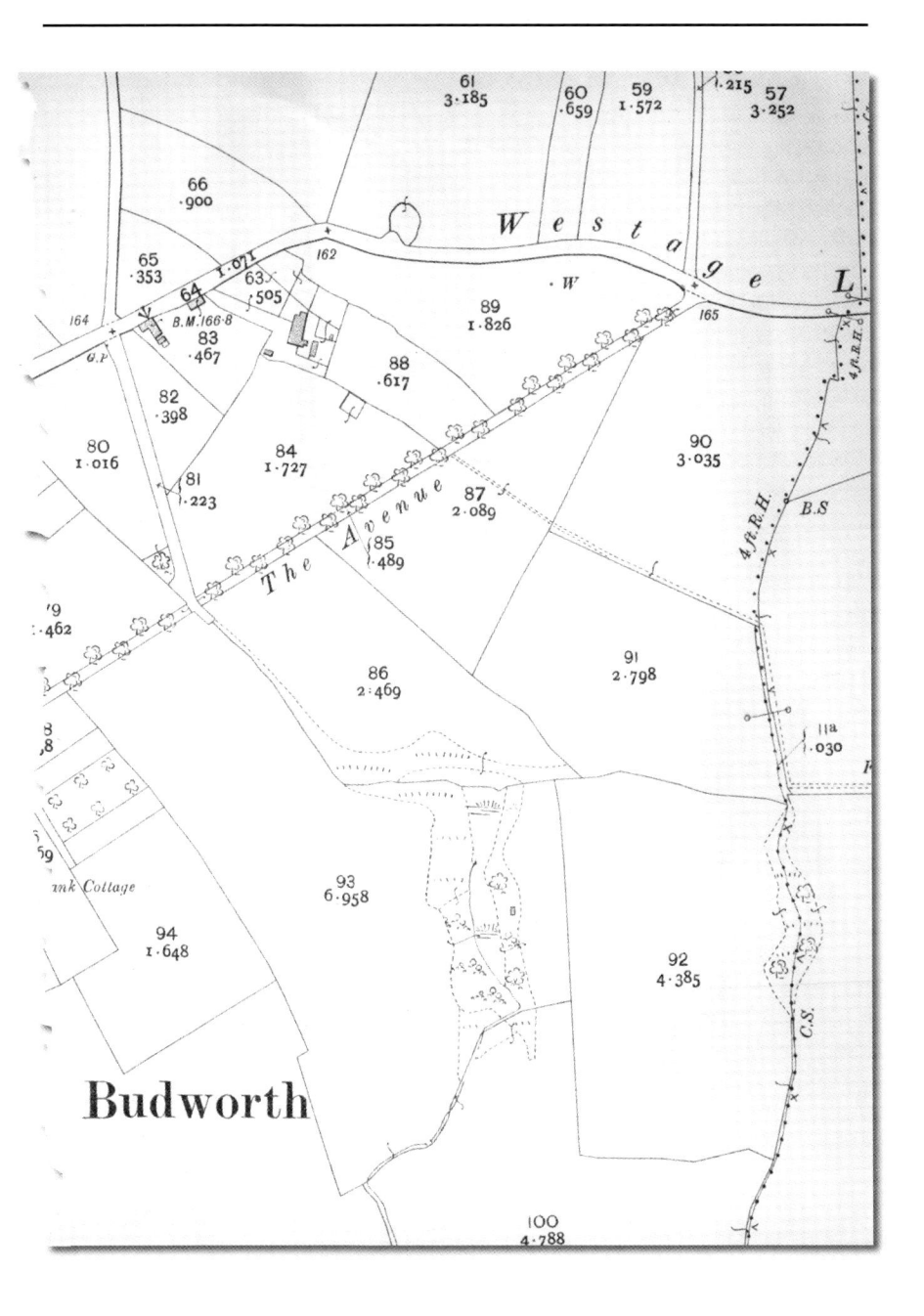

ARLEY WAKES

SEPTEMBER 8TH, 1857,

A Holiday will be granted to the Labourers and others in the employ of R. E. E. Warburton, Esq., who are willing to join in the games.

The Games will commence at Two o'clock in the Afternoon.

1st. A Race by Arley School Boys - - - **A BOOK.**
2nd. A Race by Men for - - - - - **A HAT.**
3rd. For the Man who can put the Stone furthest - **A FLANNEL SHIRT.**
4th. For the highest Leap by Arley School Boys **A CLASP KNIFE.**
5th. Pulley Hauley, five on each side - - **FIVE SHILLINGS.**
6th. For the Man who can pitch the Sledge Hammer furthest - **A SPADE.**
7th. A Wheelbarrow Race for - - - - **A BUCKET.**
8th. A Sack Race for - - - **A COUPLE OF SACKS.**
9th. For the Man who can wheel the Greatest Weight over an Incline - - - - - **A SCYTHE.**
10th. A Hurdle Race - - - - **A TEA KETTLE.**

N.B.--No Jump allowed to count where the Jumper falls. All distances measured at right angles to the line of goal. Winners of the same Prize for two previous years to be disqualified.

No one will be allowed to compete for any Prize unless he has given in his name to Mr. Donald, on or before Tuesday, the 8th of September.

ARLEY, August, 1857.